There are certain vital careers that decide the fate of the world—*a world in which each of us has a stake.*

In this latest Christopher book Father Keller discusses these careers and shows how *you*—on your own—can find openings in the vital fields of education, government, radio and television, labor relations, social service, and secretarial work.

Our "Let George do it" attitude fostered the rise of Hitler and the spread of Communism and it has encouraged the opportunist and those dedicated to subversion to get into these key fields. The Christopher thesis is: *Do something about it.* And to this end Father Keller gives thoroughly detailed information about preparing résumés, approaching employment agencies, available openings in television, educational opportunities, and an exhaustive list of government agencies.

Perhaps you yourself cannot go into any of these fields to take your part in changing the world—but there is still something you can do. You can influence those who are in them, and you can encourage others to do so. There is a part for each one of us in changing the world, and CAREERS THAT CHANGE YOUR WORLD points the way to do it.

BY JAMES KELLER

Men of Maryknoll
You Can Change the World
Three Minutes a Day
Careers that Change Your World
One Moment Please!
Government Is Your Business
Just for Today

CAREERS
THAT CHANGE
YOUR WORLD

Christopher Guides

for Jobs That Make the Future

BY

JAMES KELLER, M.M.

CHRISTOPHER BOOKS
18 East 48th Street
New York 17, N.Y.

Nihil Obstat:

JOHN M. A. FEARNS, S.T.D.
Censor Librorum

Imprimatur:

✠ FRANCIS CARDINAL SPELLMAN
Archbishop of New York

The nihil obstat and imprimatur are official declarations that
a book or pamphlet is free of doctrinal or moral error. No
implication is contained therein that those who have granted
the nihil obstat and imprimatur agree with the contents, opinions, or statements expressed.

New York, October 27, 1950.

FOREWORD

In the first Christopher* book, *You Can Change the World,* an attempt was made to underline the fact that every individual, young or old, rich or poor, highly educated or untutored, in low position or high, can play an important part, however small, under God, in changing world trends for the better.

This book endeavors to go one step further. It aims to draw attention—especially now when human beings are again dying on distant battlefields—to the fact that certain vital careers decide the fate of the world, in which each of us has a stake.

While persons of high character and competence are needed in every phase of private and public life—in the home, the church, the professions, business, the farm, the factory—in a more particular way are they needed in the great creative spheres of influence that affect the destiny, for time and for eternity, of all mankind: (1) education, (2) government, (3) communications, (4) labor relations, (5) social service, and (6) library work.

Because most of us have taken the *"Let George do it"* attitude, we have presumed that someone else would take care of everything else while we took good care of ourselves. *We have neglected these careers that count.* On the other hand, the self-seekers, the weaklings, the opportunists, and those dedicated to perversion and subversion have recognized the importance of these key fields and have been swarming into

*The word *Christopher* is derived from the Greek word, *Christophoros,* meaning *Christ-bearer.*

5

them as fast as they can. They readily see that a handful of persons, good or bad, in these vital fields can make or break any nation, can cripple the home, religion, and every other civilizing influence.

The Christopher thesis is: *"Do something about it."* Mere complaining or criticizing accomplishes little or nothing. *"Better to light one candle than curse the darkness"* sums up much of our approach. We maintain that each worker, already in any one of these careers, who is *recharged* with Christlike purpose to strive devotedly and loyally for the common good of all is a candle *relighted;* and each new person, fired with love of God and country, who is encouraged or guided to go as a Christ-bearer into even a minor post in a vital career is new light *added.*

In proportion as this simple, hopeful, constructive process is developed and speeded, so will the peace of Christ, for which all men long, be restored to a weary, desolate world. *In exact proportion as light is added, so does the darkness disappear.*

Because the saving of the world is everybody's business, because each and every one has been entrusted by God with a mission in life to leave this world a bit the better for his or her being in it, and because we have seen time and time again the far-reaching results for good that even the least individual can effect, we respectfully address this book to YOU, whoever you may be.

After all, it is *your* world, *your* government, *your* atomic energy, *your* television, *your* colleges, *your* labor problems, *your* social service as much as it is anybody's. Whether you are a housewife, a garage mechanic, a nurse, or a bus driver, you have a responsibility to your world. You are important! Even if you are far removed from any of the careers that count, still, by work and by prayer, you can do something to see that these same careers make *your* world and not break it. The more you know about these careers the more you will see the importance of having the best possible players on *your* team—those who are trying to win the game for God, not lose it to the godless. No one else can substitute or supply the contribution that you—and you alone—can make.

The more you know about these careers the more you will see how essential *your* interest in them should be. This book, with its necessary limitations, can supply only a portion of the information you should have. At best it will do little more than give you a "bowing acquaintance" with a few vital careers that we consider more important in these crucial times. In subsequent books, God willing, we hope to treat the forty other careers that count.

A deep debt of gratitude to friends, too numerous to mention, who have made much appreciated contributions to this book!*

James Keller

THE CHRISTOPHERS
18 East 48th St., N.Y. 17, N.Y.
Father James Keller, M.M., Director

Each of the chapters in this book has been divided into four parts in order that it may serve as basic material for a course of four lessons in a career-guidance school, a study club, or discussion group. We leave it to the person directing any one of these groups to expand on the limited material presented here from his or her own experience or from other authoritative sources.

CONTENTS

CAREERS THAT CHANGE YOUR WORLD

WHAT'S WRONG WITH THE WORLD
—AND WHAT YOU CAN DO ABOUT IT

1.

How It All Began

One bitter day in deep Manchuria in 1935 a young American missioner came upon a withered old native woman, miserably dressed and hollow-eyed with hunger. He led her to shelter and warmed her with hot food.

Her eyes followed him wherever he moved. She seemed deeply puzzled. Finally she blurted out what was in her mind. "Why do you bother with me when no one else cares?" she asked.

"Because God made you and God made me," the priest told her. "And He said we were to go out over the world and help all who are in need."

The old woman stared, deeply touched. She said, "What a beautiful idea! Where did it come from? Who started it?" The missioner patiently explained Christ's works among the poor and the afflicted and how He had left His followers the great command: Go out over the world and help all who suffer.

The old pagan woman pondered this a long time. Finally she said, "This Christ—He cannot be long dead?" and the missioner told her He had lived on earth nineteen hundred years before.

With childlike simplicity, she said: "Nineteen hundred years ago He commanded His followers to spread this beautiful idea of love for man—then where have you Christians been all these nineteen hundred years? Why haven't they done what Christ said?"

When I first heard this story in 1935 it disturbed my conscience. The more I thought of it the more did it appear to me that the pitiful plight of humanity today might be due far more to our failure to play our part as followers of Christ than to the activities of all the evildoers combined.

While there was much cause for shame in this, there was also cause for *hope*. The God-given opportunity for each of us to reach out to the big world in the name of Christ still remains in our hands.

The pagan woman's simple question—*"Where have you Christians been?"*—contributed in no small way to the start of the Christopher movement.

Two other happenings helped in a particular manner to bring about the launching of the Christopher idea.

One occurred when a Jewish friend, the assistant to a Broadway producer, read *Men of Maryknoll*. The book told what a handful of Maryknoll missioners accomplished, in spite of great odds, to bring physical and spiritual consolation to some of the afflicted millions in China, Japan, and other parts of the Orient. Their example, I felt, might stimulate many others to follow in their footsteps.

There was an added objective. I hoped that this book might remind thousands, in all walks of life, that each of them could also play a role in changing the world for the better. This friend, after reading the book, made a remark that increased this hope. *"These are Christians with guts! There ought to be a million more like them."*

That significant observation convinced me that a million people in all walks of life could be found to help restore the peace of Christ to the world. Each person was important; each counted. Yes, each could be an apostle, a missioner, a

Christ-bearer and play some part, no matter how small, in hastening the fulfillment of the much-neglected command of Christ: *"Go ye into the whole world; preach the gospel to every creature."*

A third compelling factor that led to the launching of the Christopher movement was the discovery, in 1944, that the Communists, with their usual proficiency, had started a new and effective lay missionary program of their own. They had begun a nation-wide string of "adult training schools," aimed at indoctrinating hundreds of thousands with a *purpose* and *direction* that had but one objective: the undermining and eventual overthrow of the United States—and all the nations of the world.

The first and most effective of these schools, the Jefferson School of Social Science, was established in New York City. On January 3, 1949, the *Daily Worker* boasted that this one school had "trained" fifty thousand students since its opening in February 1944—an average of ten thousand a year.

Those who have attended the school have pointed out that in nearly every class the teacher emphasized to all students in one way or another: *"What we give you doesn't belong to you alone. Get out and spread it. Don't take any kind of a job. Take only a job that counts, a job where you can reach the many, not merely the few. Let the rest of the people take the ordinary jobs. Get on the staff of a college, on a board of education, in a government office, in a labor union, on a newspaper, into a television station, into the writing of comic books, or any other key spot where you can reach the millions."*

A person interested in a career in television, for instance, who drifts into a Communist school for guidance or direction, gets something of television technique, of course. But for the most part he gets a few lessons in Marxism and how to apply or *integrate* it into TV. After this simple preparation, out steps the trainee, all set to go with apostolic zeal into the thick of things. Having been quickly but intensively "briefed," *he knows where he is going. He has purpose and direction. He* is miles ahead of the average person, who is almost devoid of any purpose or direction outside of taking care of himself.

Thirty-seven of these Communist schools, located across the country, were branded as "subversive" by the Department of Justice. But that didn't prevent them from continuing operations. Usually a high-sounding name, such as that of a famous American, was given them to deceive loyal citizens who, looking for adult training, unwittingly fell into the hands of the Communists for lack of any other place to go. Give the Communists their due, however. They were on the job. For evil ends they were using missionary methods that we have neglected to use for good.

A valuable technique could, therefore, be learned from them. What they were doing seemed to be another forceful reminder of a failure on our part. They had inspired countless human beings to take up CAREERS of spreading hatred and confusion throughout the world. These people were encouraged to get into every channel of influence and communication that would quickly diffuse their ideas and blend them into every facet of life. They became CAREER propagandists.

Why could not men and women who sought the love and peace of Christ for the world make similar CAREERS for themselves—in effect, become Christ-bearers or Christophers? They could dedicate themselves with even greater zeal and devotion to a lifetime of service in the careers that count and make a mighty—possibly decisive—contribution to that precious peace for which all men long. *If a few more would LIVE for peace now, million. might not have to DIE for peace in the future.*

ENCOURAGING BEGINNINGS

With these three factors urging me on, I began to experiment with the Christopher idea. The more I did, the more I began to realize that in each and every human being there is great *power for good,* a "bit of the missionary," implanted by God Himself, which needed only to be developed and

16

brought to bear on an ever-widening scale to solve many of the world's major problems.

Every attempt proved that with God's help it was easy to get people everywhere to become Christophers, or Christ-bearers; to get them to do something to bring Christ into the market place instead of sitting on the side lines, complaining or criticizing. *"Be not overcome by evil, but overcome evil by good."* (Romans 12:21)

In 1945 the Christopher movement formally swung into action. Everybody and anybody could *start* to be a Christopher, it was pointed out. The importance of the individual was stressed from the very beginning for those who would be Christophers. It was stipulated that each one participating would do so on an entirely voluntary basis. There were to be no meetings, no memberships, no subscriptions, no dues. Each was expected to stand on his own feet, to show personal initiative and responsibility, to undergo personally the valuable missionary experience of finding his own sphere of operations, to get into career work of his own choosing. It was up to each to do as much or as little as he liked.

Furthermore, we stressed that one need not necessarily be brilliant, well-trained, or in a high position. No matter how limited a person's qualifications might be, he or she could still wield far-reaching influence for good as a Christ-bearer. As St. Paul so forcefully put it: *"The foolish things of the world hath God chosen, that he may confound the wise; and the weak things of the world hath God chosen, that he may confound the strong."* (I Corinthians 1:27)

BLESSED WITH SUCCESS

God blessed the Christopher movement from the very outset. Humanly speaking, the simplicity of its approach perhaps had much to do with its success. Tens of thousands of cases could be cited illustrating how men and women in every part of the country have picked up the Christopher challenge of *"doing something"* instead of merely talking about a situation or criticizing and doing nothing. Yet the very fact that there are so many people—at least one hundred thousand—already doing Christopher work gives refreshing hope of what the future may hold in store once their number is increased to *a million or more.*

For those unacquainted with the Christopher movement we cite in brief detail a few examples of what can be done in a Christopher way to change the world for the better:[1]

1. A Kentucky businessman who wrote that he had a habit of complaining about bad government yet doing nothing about it found himself moved to action by some Christopher literature he chanced to find. He decided to run for the state legislature. Many doors were slammed in his face—but many were opened, too. He was elected. At the end of his letter to us he made just one request: *"Please pray that I do a just and honest job for my constituents."*

2. In Texas not long ago a twenty-three-year-old Baptist schoolteacher was moved to action by an article about the Christophers which appeared in the *Reader's Digest.* She said the point she liked best was the emphasis on what little people can do to change the world for the better. "You know," she said, "for the first time in my life I realized that a little person like myself counted." Then she went on to explain that she was teaching in a public school, that it was hard work, et cetera, and that most of the girls she knew were getting out of the teaching field because they felt there was not enough money in it . . . the pay was too low. "But," she added, "I'm not only going to continue teaching. I decided to become a 'committee of one' and get as many girls as I can to enter the teaching field. Incidentally, I got my first recruit yesterday!"

3. As a result of a talk on the Christophers in a Rochester, New York, hotel three years ago, seven college seniors who were present made some very decisive moves along Christopher

[1]Personal names are used in relating incidents whenever the information has already been made public. In all other instances, names have been withheld, usually at the request of the individuals concerned.

lines. One called at our headquarters recently and told us the story. He said that he and his six companions had no particular career in mind after graduation. As a matter of fact, each planned to "fall into" the first job that promised material security.

Then one day, out of curiosity, they went to hear the Christopher talk mentioned above. Throughout, the idea of *"a career with a purpose"* was stressed over and over again. The net result? All seven are well on their way *to,* or already are *in,* careers with a purpose. Our visitor told us he is preparing to be a newspaper writer. Two others are teaching in high school. Two more are taking doctorates preparatory to college teaching. The remaining two are studying for the priesthood.

4. A worker earning $62.50 a week decided to do something about improving the quality of his trade union, which had suffered much from corrupt management. He took a heavy loss in the process and used up a nest egg of one thousand dollars that he had saved toward a new home for his family. But he started a trend that has transformed the entire union.

5. A teacher at Notre Dame encouraged a student who had a bit of literary ability to make a try at the writing field upon graduation and not take just any job that came along. He warned the young man that there would be many difficulties in the beginning, that things would be hard for a new writer breaking into the field. But the teacher also pointed out the tremendous influence that writing exerts on the lives of millions the world over. He suggested that it would be worth all the time and effort and possible heartbreak to become a part of the vital sphere. The student took the advice. Today he is one of the most promising young writers in the movie industry.

6. A Polish widow who takes in laundering to support her family said she wanted to do something besides *"wash my way through life."* She decided that, in her own small way, she could help make the world a bit the better for her being in it. Accordingly, she started to offer up her daily prayers and sufferings for one of the foremost labor leaders of the

country, a man she had never met. She realized that in his hands rested the destiny of hundreds of thousands of workers. When asked why she prayed for him in particular, she quietly replied: *"Well, I don't know anyone who needs prayers more than he does."*

GET ON THE JOB

It needs no stretch of the imagination to envision the transformation that can take place over our country—and over the earth—if enough persons like the above can be found to get into the main stream of life and do something about changing the world for the better. The presence of just one Christopher in any environment, even the worst, is a blessing, a channel of grace, a candle in the darkness, a step in the right direction.

Yet it cannot be emphasized too strongly that this step must be taken on an *ever-widening scale* if we are to avert the catastrophe that becomes more threatening every day.

Encouraging as has been the spectacular growth of the Christopher movement, thanks to God, since its start in 1945, our constant fear is that we are not moving fast enough and far enough. This fear was further pointed up for us not long ago when an army officer from Washington came into our headquarters here in New York City and said something we will not soon forget.

"I am a Protestant," he stated, *"and I think you are on the right track with this Christopher idea of getting better-quality people into government and education and all the other vital fields. But you'll have to go at it on a much bigger scale and in a hurry."* He went on to say that he's convinced *"this country stands a good chance of cracking up"* within a few years. *"Communism is only one part of the trouble,"* he said. *"It is even more the moral decay that is eating into everything—corruption in high places, dishonesty, perjury, graft, immorality, breakup of home life, and disregard for ordinary decency."*

2.

Purpose Makes the Difference

Hundreds of splendid technical books have been written for those anxious to make more money or achieve greater worldly success. But few, if any, books are available that stress both the need of high motivation in the more important spheres of influence and the unusual opportunity open to an individual to enrich humanity—to leave the world a bit the better for his being in it—if, with a Christlike purpose, he goes into a career that counts.

Since, therefore, *purpose makes the difference,* it seems well at the very outset to recall briefly the basic reasons for such motivation—*the one and only reason for this book.*

Shortly after the Constitution was signed in Independence Hall, Philadelphia, on September 17, 1787, a woman approached Benjamin Franklin to ask him what the result of this would be. *"What have we got, Dr. Franklin?"* she inquired.

"Madame," Franklin replied, *"we have a republic, if we can keep it!"*

Nearly a hundred years later a somewhat similar question was put to James Russell Lowell, then American Minister to Great Britain. *"How long,"* Lowell was asked, *"will the American republic endure?"*

Lowell's answer, like Franklin's, was crisp and to the point: *"As long as the ideas of the men who made it continue to be dominant."*

Our country has come a long way in its short history of one hundred and seventy-five years. And yet at the peak of a material greatness with which no other nation has *ever* been blessed there is a feeling of inner insecurity which is spreading over the length and breadth of the land among all classes of

21

people. Too many are losing a sense of the very purpose of life.

The idea uppermost in the minds of the men who started America was that each and every human being was important because he was made in the image and likeness of God. During the last few decades there has been a gradual chipping away at this idea, followed by an aggressive attempt in our own day to replace it with the theory which considers the human being as an animal and nothing more. This trend has increased since the first World War. Today it has reached a point where it may seriously threaten our very existence as a nation if it is not checked at once. On a wider plane, it is a trend away from all the principles upon which our republic was founded . . . *and without which it cannot hope to survive.*

SIGN OF THE TIMES

In order to be prepared to tackle the task in a practical manner, each of us must recognize this downward trend, to be aware of the signs of the times, since, as the Chinese ironically say, *"Things are rapidly getting no better."* The following are a few indications:

1. *Decline in religion.* About one hundred million Americans either belong to no church or have no practical contact with one. They are spiritually adrift. They know less and less of *what they are, why they are here, where they came from, where they are going.* While living off the benefits of Christianity, they are becoming less and less aware of the very truths that make their free way of life possible. Among this one hundred million, a government investigator told us he estimates there are some five million who have been following and often defending the half-truths of Communism without realizing the harm they are doing. It is the old story: *"Those who stand for nothing easily fall for anything."*

2. *Dangerous trends in education.* For many years our schools have been neglecting to bring into the lives of millions of young Americans the basic spiritual truth which is the root of America's strength. The concept of man as being nothing more than a superior animal has been steadily fostered in

the classrooms. As Dr. Ralph Sockman, a prominent Methodist minister, put it: *"We cannot preserve Christian democracy by training our children as pagans."*

While our youth learn about many philosophies contrary to the true American thought and spirit, there is a growing lack of emphasis on our own heritage. According to the Federal Office of Education, Washington, D.C., only nine states out of the forty-eight require the teaching of the Declaration of Independence. On April 17, 1950, the New York *Times* pointed out that 66 per cent of the nation's colleges do not insist on the study of United States history despite the fact that an *"overwhelming majority"* of the country's key educators believe that *"a good grounding in our history will make students less susceptible to foreign ideologies."* As an evidence of the lack of interest even in contemporary affairs that affect our nation, at one leading women's college in California, the magazine *Time* reported, a poll taken among one hundred students taking a course in international relations disclosed the following: Seventy admitted they had no idea of what bipartisan foreign policy is, thirty-eight were *"totally uninformed"* about the Atlantic pact, nine never read the newspapers, and fifty-six merely glanced over the headlines. Even the student paper expressed its shock at the disclosure by writing: *"It costs our parents $1,550 a year, plus transportation, clothes, allowance, and incidentals, to send us here to be educated. . . . Educated for what?"*

3. *Increase of nervous disorders.* The trend in this direction is taking on epidemic proportions. Some doctors claim that over fifteen million Americans are afflicted with mental and nervous disorders. They are either in hospital or in need of hospitalization. They say that much of the trouble of the people is due to the elimination of God from their lives. Their attempt to settle inner conflicts is futile chiefly because they have no power higher than themselves to which to turn.

4. *Neglect of careers that count.* An Episcopalian minister in one of the prosperous suburbs of New York, who is much interested in the Christopher movement, gave us the follow-

ing significant information: After checking over a list of 1,796 persons who have gone through his hands during the last thirty years, he knows of only nine who have taken up careers in the vital fields of education, government, writing, and labor. He said that most of the people are in engineering, advertising, brokerage, or in various mercantile, manufacturing, and sales activities, all good and necessary in themselves but not careers that determine the course of the world.

The proportion of those going into spheres that touch the lives of all is far too small for safety. In fact, this neglect is leaving the door open to those who are ill-equipped or even hostile to God and country. An increasing number of parents actually are discouraging their sons and daughters from taking up any type of life that involves service to others. They bring them up on the principle: *"Put in as little as possible and take out as much as you can."*

5. *Corruption in public life.* The same corruption in public life that preceded the downfall of every nation from the days of Rome down to the present is corroding our very foundation. Ordinary honesty and loyalty are being disregarded on all sides. A judge in San Francisco told us that hardly anyone appearing before him believes in an oath. Men and women in important positions in government have acted as traitors in giving away precious secrets to those who would destroy our country. Graft, deliberate violation of promises, the use of an office of public trust to further one's own selfish ambitions, lack of purpose outside of one's self—these and other evidences of moral decay that seldom reach the headlines are occurring on a scale never known before in our country.

OBVIOUS CONCLUSION

The recital could go on and on, but it is obvious from this small bit of evidence that our problem is far more than Communism, dangerous as that is. The disciples of godlessness have merely been shrewd enough to use our *moral decline* for their own advantage. Communism could disappear overnight and the problem confronting us here, as well as over the world, would still be an enormous one.

The big issue, then, is much more than Communism. It is that our country—our world—is *losing its soul*. Our spiritual resistance has become so low that even if we succeed in eliminating the virus of Communism, an infection even more deadly might take its place.

This despiritualizing process, to which the weakened nature of man easily inclines, has been given special impetus by a few individuals, apostles of godlessness, during the last hundred years both here and abroad.

IT DIDN'T JUST HAPPEN

Hitler, for instance, didn't just happen by chance. He was the inevitable "product" of a pagan philosophy first set in motion by a few individuals in Germany in the middle of the nineteenth century. They influenced the intellectuals who were to be the leaders. Their aim was to eliminate all reference to God from education, science, government and all other forms of German life. And the very day they started they actually were paving the way for a Hitler, for one who would champion a deified State.

In our own country, some fifty years later, another handful undertook the same godless program. These were not Communists . . . yet they have probably shaped the trend to godlessness in America more than all other forces combined.

They frequently were men of great force and persuasion. Gifted with many attractive qualities, they were extremely disarming, won innumerable friends, and still rank today among the famous men of our time.

However, despite their pre-eminence, the fact remains that not only did they reject the fundamental idea on which our republic is founded but, even more important, *they were the means of causing millions of others to follow in the same godless path.*

TWO IN PARTICULAR

Two of these "thought molders" in particular, educator John Dewey and Supreme Court Justice Oliver Wendell Holmes, can be cited.

Dewey, the most influential and widely followed "authority" of our time in the field of education, can be considered to be the chosen leader of the forces of *secularism* in America. His philosophy of life is indicated in this statement in the May–June 1933 issue of the *New Humanist*, which he signed along with others of similar mind:

> *We regard the universe as self-existing and not created. We believe that man is a part of nature and that he has emerged as the result of a continuous process. We reject the traditional dualism of mind and body. We assert that modern science makes unacceptable any supernatural or cosmic guarantees of human values. We consider the complete realization of human personality to be the end of man's life. We are convinced that the time has passed for theism, deism, and modernism.*

In his own book, *What I Believe* (page 182), Dewey also stated:

> *Faith in the divine author and authority in which Western civilization confided, inherited ideas of the soul and its destiny, of fixed revelation, of completely stable institutions, of automatic progress, have been made impossible for the cultivated mind of the Western world.*

Dewey rejected any immutable laws and insisted that men should give up faith in God, in Christ, in the Ten Commandments, in moral principles, in any and all religion. His position in this was much the same as that of Joseph Stalin. The far-reaching influence of this one individual was pointed out some time ago in *Vogue* magazine (February 1948, page 214): "*John Dewey, a dauntless eighty-eight, is one of the pivotal thinkers of his day. He, more than anyone else, has*

*shaped the present educational path of this country, has fur-
thered the thinking of the world with his philosophy, a system
of thought 'based on experience as the ultimate authority in
knowledge and conduct.' "*

"THE SECRET OF MR. JUSTICE HOLMES"

As regards the second of the two foremost "thought molders," Harold R. McKinnon of the San Francisco Bar, writing
on "The Secret of Mr. Justice Holmes" in the *American Bar
Association Journal*, April 1950, made certain revealing observations. He pointed out that while Holmes was a man of
great personal charm, a distinguished jurist, and a persuasive
writer, yet his philosophy was *"agnostic, materialistic, hope-
less of the attainment of any ultimate truth, meaning, or standard of value. As a result it is fundamentally indistinguishable
from the amoral realism of those regimes of force and power
that are the scandal of our century. . . . His concept of man
is an instance in point. When thinking coldly, he* [Holmes]
*said he saw 'no reason for attributing to man a significance
different in kind from that which belongs to a baboon or a
grain of sand'* (*Holmes-Polloch Letters*, Vol. 2, p. 252)."

When you put the following statement of Hitler—*"To the
Christian doctrine of the infinite significance of the human
soul and of personal responsibility, I oppose with icy clarity
the saving doctrine of the nothingness and insignificance of
the human being"*—alongside the words of Justice Holmes,
the similarity is a little too close for comfort.

In the same article on Justice Holmes, Mr. McKinnon
pointed out that in the former chief justice's philosophy truth
fares no better than morals. Holmes said: *"Truth is the majority vote of that nation that can lick all the others."*

With more American soldiers dying on foreign soil, and
with the clouds of another World War looming ever darker
on the horizon, it is a sickening thought to realize that we
have been nurturing in our midst the same deadly "might
makes right" philosophy that has been the **diabolical force**

behind Communism, Nazism, Fascism, and all the other forms of atheistic militarism.

All the world has had a bitter lesson in the deadly results that are the inescapable outcome of a philosophy which reduces man to the status of a *"baboon."* But it is a problem that can be solved more surely by a positive, constructive approach than by merely beating the air and complaining about the damage these few have done.

Give the godless credit for being on the job—for accomplishing so much. Their very achievement is a forceful reminder of the refreshing change for the better that can come once there are as many working daringly *for* what the godless are working *against*.

3.

Secure These Truths

A leader of Communism in the United States told one of his assistants privately some time ago: *"All our talk about capitalism being the one big enemy of Communism is just for public consumption. Our real struggle is against religion. That is the one big obstacle in our way."*

Recent happenings over the world bear witness to this. In every country taken over by the totalitarians, the one force they quickly liquidate or strangle is *religion*. Why? Because religion is forever reminding the millions that the first allegiance of each person is to a Supreme Being Who is the Author of all life and from Whom our every human right is derived. Awareness of this one truth alone is a powerful "roadblock" to any and all who would set up a slave state.

Only recently East Germany's Communist government was reported by the Associated Press as extending into all public schools the instruction that *"Jesus Christ never existed and the Bible is a collection of myths."* The Red government realizes full well that it can never completely subjugate the minds and hearts of the people so long as they revere Christ as the Son of God.

BETTER TO BE POSITIVE

All of this should make the issue—and the solution—more clear. There is a powerful reminder in the relentless opposition to religion on the part of the totalitarian philosophies from abroad and that of the godless within our midst. Instead of using too much valuable time and effort fighting them, why not be actively *for* the truths they are so much *against?* It is just plain good business to push one's own product rather than to talk too much about one's competitor.

If the enemies of civilization work furiously to eliminate God from everything, in order to destroy our liberty, that ought to be argument enough for us to work ever more zealously to put God right back into everything.

If we had to start from scratch in this positive approach, it would be well worth every bit of struggle that it would cost. But fortunately we don't. We in America have a rich heritage that stems from a profound belief in God. It is our conviction that it would not take too much effort to focus attention on it once again—to bring it back into the forefront of American life, to make it live as a positive dynamic force in public and private affairs.

Over a hundred years ago the sage De Tocqueville wrote the following interesting comment:

"*...The Americans combine the notions of Christianity and liberty so intimately in their minds that it is impossible to make them conceive the one without the other.*"

All who are interested in rediscovering the real sources of our strength and freedom would do well to ponder at length the following facts:

CORNERSTONE OF AMERICAN LIFE

It may come as a surprise to many that *every* President of the United States from George Washington on down has paid public tribute to the fact that the cornerstone of American life rests on a strong spiritual foundation. For example, in his Farewell Address, delivered in 1796, Washington observed:

Of all the dispositions and habits which lead to political prosperity, religion and morality are indispensable supports. . . . Let us with caution indulge the supposition that morality can be maintained without religion.

A similar tribute was voiced by President Lincoln in 1858, coupled with a much-needed warning. In what Carl Sandburg, in *Lincoln Collector*, refers to as the "lost" speech of Abraham Lincoln, the great President spoke these words concerning the Declaration of Independence and the motives of those who wrote it:

This was their lofty and wise and noble understanding of the justice of the Creator to His creatures, to the whole great family of man. In their enlightened belief, nothing stamped with the Divine image and likeness was sent into the world to be trodden on and degraded, and imbruted by its fellows.

On June 7, 1950, President Truman, while addressing a convention of Lutherans in Washington, D.C., uttered these significant words:

We are faced with tremendous responsibilities. We have become the leaders of the moral forces of the world, the leaders who believe that the Sermon on the Mount means what it says, the leaders of that part of the world which believes that the law is the God-given law under which we live, that all our traditions have come from Moses at Sinai and Jesus on the Mount. . . .
We have forces in the world that do not believe in a moral code, that even go so far as to say there is no Supreme Being, that material things are all that count. Material things are ashes, if there is no spiritual background for the support of those material things.

FOUR SPECIFIC REFERENCES

The basis of the moral code to which President Truman refers is *dependence on God,* Whom we recognize as the Source of all our liberty and strength. Our Founding Fathers made four explicit references to this very fact in the immortal Declaration—the charter of our freedom!

1. In the first sentence they wrote: "*. . . to which the Laws of Nature and of Nature's God entitle them . . .*"

2. In the second sentence: "*. . . that all men are created equal, that they are endowed by their Creator with certain unalienable Rights . . .*"

3. In the next to last sentence: "*. . . appealing to the Supreme Judge of the world . . .*"

4. And in the last sentence: "*. . . with a firm reliance on the protection of divine Providence . . .*"

PROPHETIC REMINDER

About two hundred and fifty years ago, before the establishment of our republic, this same concept of recognition and reliance on the Creator of all was voiced by William Penn when the charter of the Commonwealth of Pennsylvania was being written. "*Those people,*" he said, "*who are not governed by God will be ruled by tyrants.*"

To go back even farther, through all the centuries of Christianity and for a thousand years before that—when the Jews alone kept alive the same divine concept—man has recognized that:

1. Each and every human being comes from God and must one day return to God to render an account of his stewardship.

2. He has certain fundamental rights given him by God that no power on earth can lawfully take from him.

3. The chief purpose of government is to secure these God-given rights.

ACTION NEEDED

In our day, despite the frequent affirmation of this all-important truth upon which our very survival as a nation depends, it is becoming increasingly evident that much of this is *"just talk."*

While we have dutifully continued to give lip service to our dependence on God, *we have failed to reduce it to practice,* to *integrate* it into the important spheres that affect the lives of the vast majority of people.

We are in grave danger of being hypocritical if we delay any longer to insist that this divine truth be brought to life in our government, in our schools, and in every other phase of life. Those who are devoted followers of the anti-God thesis and who insist that man is a *nobody*—just a collection of chemicals worth about $1.89—are very much on the job. They not only talk . . . they act! They leave nothing to chance. Despite what the President or anybody else says, these apostles of godlessness despise the idea of "this nation, *under* God," and are determined to change it to "this nation, *without* God."

NEED TO RE-EMPHASIZE PRIMARY TRUTHS

In 1934 Abbé Lemaître, the great Belgian physicist who collaborated with Einstein, told a small group at a dinner in Indianapolis that much of the success of the Nazis had been due to the fact that they reduced their philosophy to a few simple ideas. These, he said, they repeated over and over until the majority of the people became so familiar with them and so well disposed to them that acceptance of the rest of the Nazis' program was made comparatively easy. The abbé then went on to say that unless means were taken immediately to re-emphasize the primary truths of Christianity and restore them to the main stream of German life, one of the greatest catastrophes in all history would soon follow.

Events since have proved the correctness of this terrible forecast.

Since the consistent practice of all totalitarians—Communists, Fascists, and Nazis alike—is to concentrate on undermining, ridiculing, or eliminating *the basic truths of religion* and the principles which stem from them, those who would be

Christophers should focus particular attention on the following fundamentals:

1. The existence of a personal Triune God Who has spoken to the world.
2. Jesus Christ, true God and true man.
3. The foundation by Jesus Christ of a Church to teach all men and bring them to eternal salvation.
4. The Ten Commandments.
5. The sacred character of the individual.
6. The sanctity of the lifelong marriage bond.
7. The sanctity of the home as the basic unit of the whole human family.
8. The human rights of every person as coming from God, not from the State.
9. The right, based on human nature, to possess private property, with its consequent obligation to society.
10. Due respect for domestic, civil, and religious authority.
11. Judgment after death.

While these eleven truths are only a portion of "all things" that Christ commissioned His Church to teach "all nations," nevertheless they are the foundation on which all else depends.

PUT THEM TO USE

Little is accomplished merely by recognizing these truths, however. We must bring them to life. They must be integrated, incarnated into everyday living, especially in the great fields of influence into which the Christophers hope to guide a million persons of high purpose. Thus can be corrected the tragic error of our day which keeps the Ten Commandments in one compartment and our daily activities in the other. These truths can be blended into every phase of our living—must be blended if our freedom is to endure. Men who need water are little interested in being told of the relative merits of hydrogen and oxygen as distinct from each other. They are waiting patiently to have these elements combined so that they may obtain the precious liquid they need.

The apostles of evil don't mind a bit if we merely *talk* our convictions, wring our hands at the breakdown of faith and morals, and confine ourselves to wishful thinking. Their only fear is that someday we will begin to *practice what we preach,* that we will wake up and see how easy it would be for us to come to grips with the problem. How? By making the truth of God come alive. By carrying it into every vital field ourselves and not expecting others to do this important task for us.

"What we need," warned General Dwight D. Eisenhower, *"is a dynamic, constructive force to lead the world. . . . Except for moral regeneration, there is no hope for us, and we are going to disappear one day in the dust of an atomic explosion."*

The answer is in our hands. It is a terrible challenge, but we must face the facts. There is no other way than the way of Christ. *"I am the Way and the Truth and the Life."*

If we but strike a spark, that spark in the Providence of God may one day burst into a flame that will sweep over the earth.

4.

The Christopher Approach

In his column in the New York *Herald Tribune* recently, Joseph Alsop made this grim prediction:

We have perhaps three or four years to enjoy ourselves, if we go on with business-as-usual, politics-as-usual, and self-delusion-as-usual. The joyride, one hopes, will be very agreeable. But at the end will come a big bang, or more likely a small, self-pitying whimper. And our world, the free world of the West, will then come to an end.

From time to time similar predictions have come to our notice from various parts of the world. All of them can be wrong. We hope and pray that they are. But we would be fools to ignore them when the welfare not only of one nation *but of all mankind* is at stake.

A Frenchman in a position of great authority recently summed up the reason for this dangerous state of affairs when he said: *"I am afraid that there is scarcely one person in France who is really trying to save our country. Everyone is trying to save himself."*

Time and time again the enemies of God have shown what a few can do when the majority are apathetic. As far back as 1922, Hitler recognized the power of a small number of dedicated workers. At that time he said: *"We do not want millions of indifferent rabble. We want a hundred thousand head-strong men. Our success will force the millions to follow us! . . . A minority suffices to overthrow a state when the majority of the population has gone soft and lost its direction."*

In his book *Hitler's Rise to Power,* Konrad Heiden points out that it was not the power of the Nazis in the beginning that made their headway possible. It was rather what the rank-and-file German did *not* do. He *presumed* too often that others would take care of the big world while he remained aloof in his own little world.

The more he and others like him withdrew from the market place to concentrate on themselves, the more the Nazis hurried into every sphere. This default probably did more to contribute to the disintegration of Germany than all the efforts of the Nazis combined.

> *To a frightening degree* [wrote Heiden] *the masses themselves had lost their sense of loyalty. They looked on in silence as their political world fell into ruins, and tacitly acknowledged that a new, uncertain, but bold edifice was growing up. There was no sudden, general flocking to National Socialism but a cynical lack of resistance.*

It is our conviction that, through the Christopher approach, through a personal, individual sense of responsibility to the world itself, this unfortunate trend can be changed—both here and over the world. It is late, yes . . . but not too late to do something about it. If a handful dedicated to the hatred of God can seize the initiative and dominate the bodies and souls of hundreds of millions, surely even a small number of those fired with the love of God can achieve far more in saving the world itself.

NO "PUSH BUTTON" METHOD

However, those who would change the world for the better must take the world as it is. They must be patient, hopeful, and persevering. Obviously, a change for the better cannot be expected overnight. There is no "push button" method to guarantee success.

Furthermore, those who would be Christ-bearers must keep in mind the realization that their power lies in being exactly what their name implies: *bearers of Christ*. By His grace, Christ works through each and all who co-operate with Him. As Christ Himself has reminded us: *"Without Me, you can do nothing."* They must be ever conscious, therefore, that all they do must be rooted in divine truth, especially in the great fundamentals that are too often taken for granted. *"Unless the Lord build the house, they labor in vain who build it."*

It is on this simple basis, then, that the Christopher approach rests.

SUMMARY

A Christopher is a bearer of Christ. Individually and personally, he carries Christ into the market place. By prayer and work he strives to bring Christian principles especially into the vital fields that touch the lives of *all* people: (1) education, (2) government, (3) writing, (4) labor, (5) social service, and (6) library work. Much of the tragedy of our times is due to the fact that godless elements have swarmed into these same spheres, while the followers of Christ have remained on the side lines, doing little more than saving themselves. Complaining, criticizing, negative analyzing will accomplish little. Positive, constructive action is needed.

A Christopher spends his time *improving*, not *disproving*.

He knows that "it is better to light one candle than to curse the darkness." As soon as there are more people "turning on lights" than there are "turning them off," then—and only then—will the darkness disappear.

FEATURES OF THE CHRISTOPHER APPROACH

1. *No Organization.* There are no memberships, no meetings, no dues—no organization beyond Christopher headquarters at 18 East 48th St., N.Y. 17, N.Y.

2. *Limitations.* The Christopher movement confines itself to one phase of a big problem. It is merely an attempt to supplement, not replace, basic and essential organization. It restricts itself to emphasis on primary truths, while recognizing the importance of all the truths that flow from them.

3. *The Distinguishing Mark.* Love of *all* people for the love of God should be the distinguishing characteristic of anyone who would play the role of a Christopher. In no case should there be a return of hate for hatred. Those who would be bearers of Christ must be ready for all the ingratitude, suffering, rebuffs, and countless disappointments which the Master encountered. Each must strive to be kind while still remaining firm, to be able to disagree without becoming disagreeable. *"Love your enemies, do good to them that hate you and pray for them that persecute and calumniate you."* With this motivation, the most difficult task can become a labor of love.

4. *Emphasis on the Individual.* Because God has implanted in every human being a desire to be creative, to make a certain contribution to the peace of the world that no one else can make, the Christopher approach stresses individual initiative. Our policy is to point out elementary principles and then leave it to each person to work out his own method of blending, integrating, or incarnating the divine into the human. This allows for greater freedom, within reasonable limits, and encourages that element of originality, imagination, and enterprise which is possible only when the individual feels a personal responsibility in changing the world for the better.

5. *No Placement Bureau.* Despite repeated requests, we have

purposely refrained from setting up any placement bureau. We feel that it is better for each to go into a job of his own choosing, when and where he likes. Furthermore, we are convinced that it is an important experience in the missionary approach of the Christopher movement for such a person to go through the difficult, and often discouraging, ordeal of finding an opening in a career that counts. God blesses the very effort of trying.

6. *Dependence on God.* By the very nature of our work, a deep conviction of dependence on God, of being an instrument, however unworthy, in the hands of God, is absolutely essential. The closer one is to Christ, the more one is bound to accomplish. Competence is needed, to be sure. But ability without godliness can be a great danger even for those who have dedicated themselves to a good cause.

7. *Our Only Contact.* At present several millions over America are at least acquainted with the Christopher idea. Our aim is merely to suggest and encourage. We leave it to each individual to find for herself or himself whatever special formation or training is needed. Our only contact with all of them is through Christopher talks, literature, books, and moving pictures. Christopher books (*You Can Change the World, Three Minutes a Day, One Moment Please!,* as well as *Careers That Change Your World*) have already had a total circulation of nearly a million copies. The first Christopher movie, *You Can Change the World,* has been seen by nearly three million persons. Plans are under way to produce twenty-nine other movies.

8. *Career Guidance Schools.* Any group may start a Career Guidance School even on a small scale and use this book or *You Can Change the World* as a basic text. However, entire responsibility for and control of each school rests with those who undertake its establishment. All that we can authorize is the material that we publish in our Christopher books or literature.

9. *No Christopher Clubs.* Because we restrict ourselves to developing individual initiative and personal responsibility, *we do not authorize Christopher clubs or groups of any kind,*

or the use of the Christopher name in connection with any project that has resulted from the Christopher idea. We leave it to each to decide whether he will work alone or join any one of hundreds of excellent organizations. Each individual speaks and acts for himself, not for the Christopher movement.

10. *Financial Support.* In keeping with our policy of no memberships, no subscriptions, no dues, we merely announce our needs, while soliciting funds from no one. We depend entirely on God to provide, through voluntary contributions, the five hundred thousand dollars a year now needed for our various Christopher projects.

11. *The Christopher Position.* The purpose of the Christophers is to restore the love and truth of Christ to the market place. Begun under Catholic inspiration, the Christopher movement has the voluntary support of hundreds of thousands of Americans of all faiths and in all walks of life. Nearly a quarter of a million of such people have individually requested that they be sent our monthly *Christopher Notes,* which are available to all, free of charge.

Inasmuch as the movement has no memberships and no meetings, each person participates in the work of the Christophers as far as he can and will.

When the first Christopher Literary Awards were made in 1949, our top prize of fifteen thousand dollars was given to George Howe, an Episcopalian, for his first novel, *Call It Treason,* which became a best seller.

An outstanding example of the widespread interest in the Christopher movement was seen in the spontaneous support given by well-known movie stars and personalities in producing the first Christopher movie, *You Can Change the World,* which tells the story of the movement. The following gave their services freely: Eddie "Rochester" Anderson, Jack Benny, Ann Blyth, Bing Crosby, Paul Douglas, Irene Dunne, William Holden, Bob Hope, and Loretta Young, as well as Leo McCarey, director, and William Perlberg, producer.

HOW YOU[1] CAN GET A JOB
WITH A PURPOSE

1.

A Goal Worth Striving For

A senior at St. John's University in Brooklyn, who had majored in English and had been on the school paper, decided to make an early start in finding an opening in the newspaper field. Having a Christopher purpose in wanting to leave the world a bit better than he found it, he felt sure God would bless him

---

[1]Throughout this book we refer to *you*. And we really mean *you*, whoever you may be, since it is *your* world and anything that concerns its destiny in these crucial times will affect you sooner or later. Whether you are a doctor, a farmer, a cook, or a stevedore, there is something you can do to change the world for the better. You may never enter one of the *careers that change your world*, but the more you know about them, the more you will talk about them and the more apt you are to become a "committee of one" to encourage others to go into them. If you are already working in one of these vital careers, perhaps this book may help to intensify your sense of purpose and so add new meaning and drive to what might have been humdrum, monotonous work when performed without a Christlike motivation. So whenever you see *"you"* in this book, for the moment try to picture yourself working in federal government, television, atomic energy, or in any other vital sphere.

for trying. And even if he failed, he would have the satisfaction of knowing that at least he had made the effort.

During his final year at college he got a job on a large metropolitan daily as a copy boy from 4 P.M. to midnight. In his spare time he practiced news writing. One day a man who did some minor writing on the paper died suddenly, and the young Christopher volunteered to try to fill the vacancy. The editor wasn't too enthusiastic, but because no one else was around he gave the lad a chance. The ex-copy boy surprised him by doing a better job than his predecessor, so the job was his . . . but not for long. An economy wave hit the newspaper and ten writers were dropped, our young friend among them.

Starting all over again, he went to another newspaper and took the only job available—opening mail. While there, however, he heard that a leading television station wanted a copy boy. He applied for and secured the job.

At night on his new assignment, while picking up coffee for the staff writers, he would often hear them bemoan the fact that they had two or three more pages to finish on a script for the following day. He lost no time in volunteering to take a try at finishing the uncompleted story. At first he wasn't very successful, but repeated practice plus a driving determination had such an effect that within a month he was given a job on the writing staff of the station!

For him—as for thousands of others—purpose indeed made the difference. For him, also, after a lifetime of service to the common good, will come the satisfaction which one man, an editor of one of the country's leading dailies, experienced as he rounded out a career of forty years as a newspaperman. During this time he had averaged forty hours a week, or two thousand hours a year, at his job—a total of eighty thousand hours spent in enriching the lives of others as well as his own.

He entered the field purposely shortly after his graduation from college because he saw in it an occupation where he could do more than earn a living. He felt he should be creative and reflect into the lives of as many as possible the blessings God had bestowed upon him. Now, as he nears the end of his career, he can feel a deep sense of gratification in knowing that the high purpose and devotion which have always characterized his work have been the means of influencing the lives of millions the country over.

Obviously, things don't always turn out as they did for these two people. But when jobs are scarce and the effort to secure them has to be made anyway, why not try for a job that counts? You may be sure that God will bless those who make the attempt at being the instruments of His Will.

GET A MILLION LIKE THEM

The examples just cited are only two of the thousands that could be told. Each is about ordinary people, young and old, rich and poor, educated and uneducated. Each shows clearly the extraordinary power for good that millions of average men and women possess.

Already there are approximately one hundred thousand Christophers making their voices heard in the places that count. But at least a *million* are needed, and needed urgently, to help avoid the catastrophe that has already engulfed half the globe.

Imagine what a refreshing change for the better will take place once this million gets into "circulation," bringing their power for good into the thick of things. By God's grace, we can have the most wonderful peace the world has ever experienced.

If they fail to serve, however, there is every reason to believe that they will be contributing, at least indirectly, to the most terrible disaster the world has ever known.

IT CAN BE DONE

Every once in a while, of course, we hear some well-disposed person argue that he or she cannot take up Christopher work in one of the main fields of influence—education, government, labor relations, communications, social service, or libraries—because he or she "just isn't cut out for that kind of work."

The fact of the matter is that there is every reason to believe that he or she will be suited to that kind of employment.

Psychologists have pointed out that there are some twen[ty]
thousand different jobs and that anyone can adapt himself [to]
a large number of them if he wishes to do so.

Then, too, many persons get discouraged after making a few calls for a job, or writing three or four letters, or dropping in at a few placement agencies. They get depressed when they see that the competition is stiff, that in some careers which count there are often fifteen or twenty persons looking for a job where there is only one opening. They give up too soon.

One experienced job consultant claims that the average experienced man or woman in a large city who is looking for a position probably sees more than one hundred employers and writes one hundred and fifty letters before securing a job. We ourselves know of an instance where four hundred persons replied to a "want ad." We also know that the one who got the job secured it not only by possessing the proper qualifications but because he persisted in trying when all his friends told him he didn't have a chance.

A young lady blessed with similar purpose and perseverance decided to put her Christopher motives to work in the writing field and started "making the rounds." The results at first, however, were anything but encouraging. In fact, after calling at no less than twenty employment agencies, with discouraging results, she decided to make one more try before giving up the idea entirely. Whispering a quick prayer, she went to the twenty-first agency. There she was told that there was no opening on any editorial staffs; however, a receptionist was needed at one of the largest publishing houses in the country if she was interested. She accepted the job without hesitation, knowing that in the Christopher approach the important thing is to "get in," no matter what the work involved. She realized that the very presence of a follower of Christ in any sphere means that he or she can be a channel of grace.

Within three weeks her writing ability was discovered by her employers. Today she is on the editorial staff in an important job and has some voice in deciding what hundreds of thousands of persons will read.

FIRST THINGS FIRST

Since it is obvious that the matter of getting a job with a Christopher purpose is a serious business, your efforts to get such a job will have to follow along the lines laid down by competent authorities in the job-placement field. However, before you set out to do your bit in helping to change the world for the better, it is suggested that you do one very important thing: *say a prayer to the Holy Spirit for guidance.*

THE ECONOMIC FACTOR

You should be prepared to make certain sacrifices should the occasion warrant it. Getting a job with a Christopher purpose will sometimes involve difficulties which would not ordinarily be present if your main concern were simply *"How much money can I make?"* Yet by no means does this imply that your economic position need be hazardous to the point where it threatens the peace and security of either yourself or your family. The best way to insure that you are properly safeguarded is to analyze your qualifications and special talents *honestly* and *objectively.*

All your talents, be they few or many, are given you by God. It follows, therefore, that you should endeavor to use them to the best advantage. To drift with the tide and take the first job that comes along undoubtedly is far easier than planning for a career which will demand more of your time and effort and best abilities. But this should *not* be the approach of those who would be Christophers.

KNOW YOURSELF AND YOU KNOW YOUR JOB

In going about getting a job in an intelligent and systematic manner, the first thing you should do is learn all about yourself—facts about your abilities, the things you are good at and the ones in which you are less proficient, which activities suit your talents and which do not. Also, so far as you are able, make a conscientious effort to evaluate your personal characteristics with this end in view: how well equipped are you to adapt yourself to some new occupation?

Analyzing yourself, then, is the first step in making plans for your future career. Naturally, if God has endowed you with only one talent, He doesn't expect you to act as if you have ten. On the other hand, if He *has* blessed you with ten talents, you have an obligation before Him to use them. One day you will have to render an account of your stewardship.

THE NEXT STEP

Secondly, try to single out the various occupations in the main spheres of ideas which interest you most. Gather all possible information and facts about these occupations, such as the *educational requirements, training, income, working conditions,* and *future opportunities.*

Once this is done, match the information you have gathered about these occupations with the information you have gathered about yourself. In this way you can discover which occupations or areas of work in the vital fields offer the best chance of worth-while results as far as you are concerned.

If, as sometimes happens, you still are undecided as to what field of influence to enter, it might be advisable to take an aptitude test given by a reputable institution organized for that purpose. To some degree a test of this sort will determine your interests. Your interests, in turn, will indicate the kind of work to which you will be most suited.

YOU STILL HAVE A CHANCE

Those who have already settled down in life may find it difficult to transfer to fields of activity where there is great need of apostolic action. However, there are tens of thousands of men and women over the length and breadth of this country who still are in a position to play an important part, individually and personally, in the fields where the fate of our country and our world may well be decided.

If you feel you are in this group, then already you realize the need for haste in getting sufficient numbers of the "missioners of light" to offset the promoters of darkness. In this struggle between God and the forces of those who hate Him, the issue is clear. As the zealous lay apostle, G. K. Chesterton, observed so well just before his death in 1936: "*It* [the struggle] *is between light and darkness, and everyone must choose his side.*"

IN YOUR POWER

It is in *your* power to bring Christ back to the world and the world back to Christ. God has put some of his own power into your hands, for He has work He wants you—and no one else—to do.

Moreover, the reward He promises is great indeed: "*Come ye blessed of my Father, possess you the Kingdom prepared for you from the foundation of the world.*"

This subject of how to get a job with a Christopher purpose will be discussed in more detail in the next, and subsequent, sections. For the moment, however, suffice it to repeat what was emphasized at the beginning of this discussion; namely, that the uppermost thought in your mind should be: "How shall I best serve God and my fellow man?" Such a consciousness will serve to sweep away a lot of objections that may arise when you begin to consider a career with a Christopher purpose.

Those with real ambition to do good have ringing constantly in their ears the challenge of urgency so well expressed in the words:

I shall pass through this world but once. Any good, therefore, that I can do, or any kindness that I can show to any fellow creature, let me do it now. Let me not defer it or neglect it, for I shall not pass this way again.

2.

Draw Up Your Balance Sheet

There is a story told about three laborers who were working on a cathedral some time ago.

The first man was a colorless individual, and when asked to define his job, he replied in a bored tone of voice: *"I cut blocks of stone . . . and let me tell you, if I didn't have to earn a living for myself and family I'd quit in a minute."*

The second man's job was to cut the timber that went into the building's construction, and he, too, found no joy in what he was doing, as was evident from his apathetic attitude and his constant complaining.

The third laborer, however, sang and whistled at his work, though he was the least skilled of the three and merely carried the stone and wood which the others prepared. None of his fellow workers could understand his zest and spirit, and one day a newcomer finally put into words the question that was on everyone's lips. *"What kind of work do you do?"* was the way he put it. *"What is your job?"*

The cheerful laborer's reply was short and simple, yet it stressed the true perspective of all his toil. *"What am I doing?"* he repeated. *"Why, I'm building a cathedral!"*

And, in truth, he *was* building a cathedral. While his role in the whole project was menial, still he was a vital factor. The structure couldn't rise without him—or someone like him. Because he had a big perspective, that perspective gave a *big* meaning to his *little* job. The same perspective should be possessed by every Christ-bearer.

To go about the task of getting a job with a Christopher purpose, it is important to draw up *your personal balance sheet.*

It has been seen that an honest, objective examination of

yourself and the field (or fields) which interests you most is of first importance in planning for a career. It follows that this information, to be of lasting practical value, should be recorded. Such a record will constitute your personal balance sheet. It will be your ready reference whenever the need arises, especially prior to your actual entry into a new occupation in one of the spheres of ideas where those who would destroy our God-given liberties are penetrating in ever-increasing numbers.

HOW TO GO ABOUT IT

You may organize the information in any form you wish. The following headings are suggested, however, inasmuch as competent authorities in the job-placement field have indicated that to group the required information under these headings will eliminate the possibility of confusion and duplication.

PERSONAL DATA

Your physical characteristics and material circumstances may affect the kind of job you want to undertake as a Christopher. It is necessary, therefore, to take into consideration such things as:

    a. Age
    b. Marital status
    c. Physical defects or handicaps
    d. General health
    e. Level of energy

Next you should try to work out some estimate of your
MENTAL ABILITIES

In order to make accurate entries here, it is often helpful to take aptitude tests, so as to measure better your mental functions. These tests, in turn, will help you evaluate your

    a. Ability to understand ideas expressed in words
    b. Reasoning powers
    c. Ability to speak
    d. Ability to write

These tests will also be a guide as to what your *interests* are, whether they be

    a. Mechanical
    b. Scientific
    c. Literary
    d. Artistic
    e. Public welfare (social service, et cetera)
    f. Educational
    g. Administrative

PERSONAL ADJUSTMENT

Next there is the matter of personal adjustment. This consideration, as well as the three previous groupings, may seem at first glance academic in the problem of getting a job. Competent job-placement specialists do *not* view them in this light. They can point to innumerable cases where a proper approach, such as is listed here, revealed talents and aptitudes in persons which those persons themselves never imagined they possessed. These people who were so helped were not necessarily failures in the particular occupations in which they were engaged. They were not, however, using their capabilities to the fullest possible extent.

For you who would approach a career with a Christopher purpose in mind, it is doubly important that you try to use the talents God has given you in the way God meant them to be used.

WHY 60 PER CENT WERE DROPPED

Even granted that one has a Christopher motivation, personal adjustment still is a factor to be reckoned with in planning a career. An employment division of one of the major industrial concerns of the country recently published a summary of the causes leading to the discharge of employees over a ten-year period. Sixty per cent of those discharged were let out because of *"poor adjustment to fellow workers."* This means that three fifths of those who lost their jobs did so because they were unable to get along with other people.

What is even more pathetic, most of those discharged blamed *someone else* for their failure. You should, therefore, make a genuine effort to arrive at the answers to such questions as:

1. Do you like people?
2. Do you feel that people like you?
3. Do you usually feel optimistic and friendly?
4. Are you able to concentrate?
5. Do you like to read?
6. Did you succeed in your studies?
7. Are you quick to praise?
8. Are you too quick to criticize?
9. Are you able to learn and profit from the mistakes of others?
10. Can you carry responsibilities?
11. Can you disagree with others without being disagreeable?
12. Are you confirmed in your Christopher purpose and goal in life?

The answers to these questions will go a long way toward determining your ability to adjust yourself to a job with a Christopher purpose. In this connection, too, it is advisable that you consider your *past achievements and failures*. Try to discover the reasons for them. Ask yourself if you have changed so that under the same circumstances you would succeed or fail, or would you react in exactly the same way as before. Did you lack perseverance, imagination, training, direction? Would you do better in similar situations in the future?

Finally, on your personal balance sheet you should list in detail the various courses which you have taken. Arrange the information under the headings:

1. Schools and colleges
2. Specialized training
3. Professional education
4. Degrees and honors

All of these details should be attended to with care. The more conscientious you are, the better the results will be. You should be ever on the alert to "follow through" this program with *action* and not merely talk about what you are going to do sometime in the future. As one letter to us recently observed: *"A friend of mine said something to me tonight that made me angry, not with her but with myself, because what she said was true. Somehow we started talking about the condition of the world, and as usual I got rather upset. My friend accused me of being an old windbag, one of those people who are always complaining but never doing anything. The trouble is . . . I want to do something, but I don't know where to start!"*

Then, too, you should be constantly on guard against the temptation of belittling your own abilities. Many people say, "Oh, but I only know one field. I've been doing this job for years . . . it would be next to impossible for me to change over now."

In some respects this may be true. There are some who would find it just about impossible to change their occupations. Yet experience and psychology both disprove the theory that an individual can fit into only one specific kind of work. The fact is that the normal individual, with average intelligence or better, is versatile and will not find it too hard to adjust to a new line of work. Will not find it too hard, that is, *if his purpose and interest are sincere.*

LET THEM KNOW

Furthermore, besides planning for a job with a Christopher objective, there is one other important way to enter a chosen field—one not usually listed when job information is given out. *Statistics have shown that the best way to get a job is to let as many persons as possible know that you are looking for a specific position.* A check of more than thirty thousand job seekers showed that approximately 30 per cent of them found jobs through contacts and suggestions from friends and acquaintances. Another 12 per cent to 14 per cent found leads through parents and relatives.

Make as many personal contacts as possible. Go out and talk to people employed in the fields in which you are interested.

Ask their advice. You'll be amazed at how many will go out of their way to help you once they see that your request is intelligent and sincere.

Apply directly to some particular "place" in the field which interests you—some special branch of government, for instance, or a publishing house, or a newspaper, an educational institution, et cetera. And don't let distance be a barrier. The job in the field you want may be three thousand miles away. If it is, exhaust every possible means to locate there. Follow the example of the usher at the Strand Theatre in New York City some years ago, who became increasingly affected by the frequent comments he heard from the movie audiences regarding the poor quality of film fare.

One day this usher decided to "do something about it." He made up his mind to give up his job, go to Hollywood, and see if there wasn't something—no matter how small—that he could do to encourage the wholesome type of entertainment he knew the movie-going public wanted. He worked his way to the film capital, and after making the rounds of the studios, day in and day out, he finally landed a job as a messenger on one of the big motion-picture lots. Because he was inspired with a high purpose, it wasn't long before he started to move ahead. He became a writer; then a production head. Every one of the films on which he worked, moreover, has proved a money-maker while still adhering to the highest standards of quality.

Remember! Don't sit back and wait for your ship to come in. Go out and meet it! Get out and make a diligent effort to find the spot in which you can do the most good.

CONSIDERING AN OCCUPATION

Now that you have analyzed yourself and drawn up a Personal Balance Sheet, you should be ready to proceed to the next step—that of learning as much as possible about the occupation that interests you. Among the most important things you should know before making up your mind are the following:

The Nature of the Work
  a. What are the activities, duties, and responsibilities of the worker?
  b. What special abilities are required?

Education and Training
  a. What educational qualifications are called for?
  b. What special training? And experience?

Entrance to the Occupation
  a. What is the best way of getting this kind of job?
  b. Would an employment agency be of help?
  c. Are there any restrictions affecting entrance or advancement in the occupation? What are they? Can they be overcome?

Evaluation of the Occupation
  a. Does the job offer an opportunity to work with a Christopher purpose?
  b. Does it offer a means of livelihood?
  c. Is there an active demand for new workers, with opportunities to do great good?

A careful study of an occupation—any occupation—before you make too much preparation for it, can save you from future disappointment, frustration, and dissatisfaction. Go for a job that best suits your abilities, interests, and temperament —though always with a Christopher purpose in mind—and the chances are you will succeed better in fulfilling the command of Christ to "go" and keep "going" with His message of love to all mankind.

3.

Match Yourself with the Job

Judith Crist, writing in the New York *Herald Tribune*, had this to say about job-getting in general and the chances open to those with adaptability and perseverance:

Industry personnel workers and employment agency officers agreed that a willingness to take a job away from home; an appreciation that beginners' wages are returning to normal; a compromise in the exact field of specialization, and an eagerness, in the last analysis, to take even a makeshift job until something better comes along—will make the search easier.

Having drawn up a list of your qualifications and a list of those qualifications required for the job at which you intend to aim, you will have succeeded in getting reasonably accurate answers to such questions as:

1. How do *your* qualifications measure up to those required by the job?
2. Are there some qualifications that you do *not* seem to have?
3. Are there some qualifications that you have but which could bear strengthening?

Also, you will have clarified in your own mind those *interests* which, as we have previously pointed out, help to guide one toward his career.

Arriving at the answers, however, will be only part of your job campaign. In addition to your interest in a particular field and your qualifications for it, you must have the capacity to do the work and carry the responsibilities called for. The better part of wisdom, therefore, would seem to dictate that you give careful consideration to several *alternate* careers before you make your final decision. It may save you needless disappointment later on.

Also, in this connection, it might be advisable that, whenever possible, you get some *preliminary experience*. Offer to do some volunteer work, if it is at all feasible. By so doing you may be able to appraise your own abilities more accurately and, at the same time, you will be able to learn what opportunities exist in a particular field.

The responsibility for choosing whether or not you will seek out a career with a Christopher objective, of course, is *yours alone*. But rest assured that if you go "one foot" of the way, God will supply the other "two feet" and help you succeed in one way or another.

FINDING THE JOB

So far everything that we have discussed can be classified as the basic "preliminaries" to the actual operation of *finding a job*.

You find a job either by locating an existing vacancy or, less frequently, by creating one where none exists but where it has been demonstrated that a need is present. You have to know where the jobs are most likely to be available before you can make an effective effort to secure one. There is no use trying to catch fish when you are miles away from the water.

Therefore, build up a list of leads and contacts which you think may be of use in pointing the way to job opportunities. Copy that list on index cards and start your own "Job Possibilities" file. Relatives and friends are often the best immediate sources of clues to occupation opportunities. Ask them to keep an eye open and, whenever possible, to make inquiries. Get as many friends as you can to be "eyes" and "ears" for you. They may learn of a vacancy or hear of an opportunity before you do. Sometimes the most unlikely leads turn up with a job opening that really offers a wide scope for Christopher action. *Don't leave any stone unturned!*

Read the "want ad" sections of newspapers. Register with a number of employment agencies. Whenever possible, register also with your school or college placement office.

Consult the classified telephone directory for the names of the firms engaged in the field of work that particularly interests you. Apply directly to these firms and, if you can, contact employees of these firms. These employees, in turn, may be able to supply you with firsthand information about their employers.

And—this is most important—go beyond your local area if no opportunities exist for the type of Christopher job you have in mind.

When you have gathered this information, under your "Job Possibilities" list you should include the names, addresses, and telephone numbers of the firms you have contacted. Also indicate on your list the name of the relative, friend, or acquaintance who gave you the lead—if any. On each card you should likewise indicate the results of any correspondence or interviews you may have had with the representatives of the various companies. This information will be a ready reference for future use and also a means whereby needless duplication and the attendant confusion may be avoided.

THE LETTER OF APPLICATION

To get a *personal* interview with your prospective employer is of first consideration in the actual process of getting a job. The personal interview is decisive. It determines in large measure whether or not you will be employed.

There are a number of ways to obtain an interview. Three of the time-tested ways are the following:

a. Telephone for an interview.

b. Let a mutual friend make an appointment for you.

c. Write your prospective employer a specific letter of application.

As you will probably have more use for the *letter of application* than any of the other ways of getting an appointment, it is necessary to examine the *three* basic letters of this type.

a. One that has been suggested by a person known to your prospective employer. This letter should start with the phrase, *"At the suggestion of . . ."*

b. One that has been suggested by a placement agency's "want ad" or an employer's direct notice in the daily newspapers. In this case the letter should state specifically the source which prompted its being written. If you are answering a direct "ad" of some firm, clip out the "ad" and attach it to the letter.

c. An unsolicited letter.

MAKE YOUR LETTER STAND OUT

If any one of these types of letters succeeds in its objective—that of getting an interview with a prospective employer or his representative—it will have taken you a considerable distance toward actually "lining up" your future career. But for such a letter to achieve worth-while results will not be easy. You will need to exercise great care. Your letter must stand out from the many your prospective employer will receive. It must reflect, as far as possible, your own personality. It must show that you are a solid and dependable type of person. It must excite his interest—at least to the point where he will want to meet you. In short, it must "sell" you.

REMEMBER THESE "12"

Your letter, then, must:

1. Be sincere. Let your letter show you off to the best advantage. State facts.

2. Be yourself. Write as you would talk to a person.

3. Be neat. Use a typewriter. Watch your spacing and don't crowd the material.

4. Be as brief as possible. Use only *one* side of the paper. Say all you have to say on *one* page.

5. Aim your letter at the employer to whom you are writing. Slant it to his special needs and policies.

6. Apply for a definite job. Don't just say that you want to work for the company.

7. Reflect confidence in yourself to do the job in question.

8. Ask for an interview. State the date and time you will be available. If necessary, give a choice of dates and time.

9. Make the matter of arranging an interview as easy as possible for your prospective employer. Sometimes it is advisable to enclose a self-addressed postcard on which he can indicate when an interview may be arranged.

10. Make certain that your name, address, and telephone number are in the letter.

11. Make a carbon copy of your letter, so that, at a later

date, you will be able to refresh your memory as to what you wrote in it.

12. Write several drafts of the letter before you decide upon a final one.

THE DRIVING FORCE

This approach should help greatly in the matter of getting a job with a Christopher purpose. But above all else your *motivation* will be the real driving force—the thing that counts! No matter what your limitations, your deep conviction that, by God's grace, you can be an instrument in bringing Him to men and men to Him will develop in you an ever-increasing missionary imagination and enterprise which constantly will lead you on to new and greater achievements.

This healthy, divine discontent will increase within you a growing resourcefulness and alertness, a keenness of observation, and a capacity for work which might have lain dormant and undeveloped if the greater cause had not lifted you out of all the depressing smallness and self-torture of concentrating only on self.

More literally than anyone else, you will experience the real *joy of living*. Life itself can take on a new and exhilarating meaning. As we emphasize over and over again, you will have the thrill of knowing that, in however small a measure, you are building, not destroying; spreading love, not hate; light, not darkness. You will be fulfilling, in the most literal sense and to the fullest possible degree, the purpose for which you were created: *to love God above all things and your neighbor as yourself.*

4.

It Makes All the Difference

In the Christopher mailbag some months ago was a letter from a well-known lawyer who had this to say about the importance of getting a job with a Christopher purpose: *"During almost twenty years of schooling, I don't recall one instance where anyone suggested to me alternatives for lifework and their various degrees of desirability. . . . Get your Christophers before they take any old job that comes along."*

The sooner this is done, of course, the better it will be both for our country and for the world. It is never too early to begin to think of a career in terms of how you can better the lot of mankind. In high school and college you can lay the groundwork for a lifetime of service to your God and your fellow man. One student at the University of California at Los Angeles, well aware of what we are trying to accomplish, put it this way: "Most people find it hard to believe how bewildered the average student is as he looks out on the world, wondering what to do with his life. Yet just a push in the right direction by someone like you Christophers can make all the difference in the world. There's a whole lot we young people can do. The sooner we get at it, the better it will be for everyone concerned."

THE RÉSUMÉ

Now that you have written your letter of application, you should prepare a résumé or data sheet for your prospective employer. It will show him that you are the type of person needed in his organization, that you have the education and experience to do a good job. For each prospective employer you should write a different résumé, since the needs of each are somewhat different.

The résumé should *not* contain a detailed statement of your entire life. It should *not* be as complete as the personal balance sheet that you have already prepared. Select from that list only those items related to the job in question. If you make a point of saying that you can do *too many things,* the chances are the employer may feel that you are a Jack-of-all-trades and master of none.

Specifically, your résumé should include the following information, though not necessarily in this order:

PERSONAL DATA: Name, age, marital status, dependents, personality traits.

EDUCATION: Academic training and special courses, particularly those designed to fit you for the job you seek.

EXPERIENCE: Mention any experience you may already have had in the particular field you intend making your career. Or mention any experience in those fields *allied* to it.

INTERESTS: List any interests which relate to the job. Only mention them at the interview, however, if the occasion arises.

DECORATIONS AND CITATIONS: If you have received any honors, for war or other service, state them. The same goes for any recognition which may have come your way for scholastic work or community and civic endeavor.

REFERENCES: Give names, addresses, occupations of persons who have known you over a reasonable period, people who have had a chance to observe you, your character, your abilities. And make certain that you have received permission from these people *before* you mention them as references.

Make a carbon copy of all this information and keep it for yourself. Take it with you to the interview, so that you will be able to refresh your memory should this be necessary.

As to *how* this information should be set forth to make the most effective presentation of your case, it is suggested that you consult any one of the many authoritative books and pamphlets on the subject. One such book, *How to Get the Job You Want*, by Lawrence Terzian (Grosset & Dunlap, publishers, $1.00 per copy), contains a wealth of information about layout, letters of application, et cetera, which should prove especially helpful.

THE INTERVIEW

The big moment in your job campaign—and it is a campaign, make no mistake about that—is the *interview*.

Prepare for it. From friends of yours, or from employees of the company, office, school, or publishing house where you would like to work, find out as much as you can about the person who is going to interview you. Go over your story; make certain you know it well. Dress conservatively and neatly. Put yourself in the employer's position and ask yourself: *What would an employer want of a prospective employee?*

Remember, he is not operating a charity. You are going to cost him money, and he has a right to expect full value in return. You have to convince him that you will be a valuable asset to his organization. When the opportunity presents itself, be prepared to stress this very point.

Before the actual interview there undoubtedly will be one or two introductory steps which will take immediate precedence. Very probably you will be met by a secretary or receptionist. In response to her questions, be courteous and pleasant. Then, if you are asked to fill out a questionnaire, do so willingly, no matter how many you may already have written.

During the actual course of the interview, present your qualifications as well as you can and, in the event this particular meeting fails to produce a job for you, try to learn of any job "clues" for the future.

THE JOB'S THE GOAL

Be yourself. Be straightforward. God expects you to be honest and conscientious under all circumstances. Make no claims that you are not able to back up. Remember, also, that an interview calls for *listening* as well as talking. Pay the interviewer the compliment of showing that you think his ideas merit your attention.

His task is to obtain certain specific facts about your qualifications. He wants to know if you have initiative, if you have personality characteristics and attitudes that will help you fit into the organization. He wants to know, also, if you are anxious to "put in" as well as "take out." Do your best to satisfy him that you are.

As the interview nears its end, as quickly as possible go over your strong points, summarizing them briefly. Clarify any matters you think may need additional explanation. Then, when the interview is over, express your pleasure at meeting the interviewer, thank him, and leave. If the decision to hire you is to be made at a later date, find out the date. If another interview is to take place with some other person, find out the date of that scheduled meeting.

Finally, don't stay a moment more than is necessary. Your time is, or should be, valuable. The interviewer's time is no less so.

It is always advisable to leave a copy of your résumé with the interviewer, so that he can consult it. A young woman we know got a job with a leading publishing concern because she took just this precaution. She had been among several applicants interviewed and had been more or less "lost in the shuffle." However, because she left a copy of her résumé with the interviewer, her name and abilities were recalled to his mind when an opening for a person who could speak French (one of her qualifications) occurred in the firm. He put through a telephone call to her, asking her to come in and see him again. And the result was she got the job.

REVIEW OF THE INTERVIEW

ANALYZE YOUR MISTAKES

If, for some reason, the interview does *not* result in a job, you should go over everything that happened at the meeting, in order to determine just how and why you failed. And profit from your failures. Remember—not everyone lands a position at the very first attempt. But remember, also, that as a Christopher you should not fall into the error of taking failures too seriously. God blesses in one way or another those who try. Seldom, if ever, does He bless moral stagnation. Also, failures are frequently blessings in disguise. They often show detours to be avoided. In your task of getting a job in order to bear Christ into the market place, you should expect difficulties. But if you depend more on God and less on self, you will be able to overcome them. As St. Paul said, we are *"not sufficient to*

hink anything of ourselves, as of ourselves, but our sufficiency
s from God."

PREPARE FOR THE NEXT INTERVIEW

Prepare yourself, therefore, for the *next* interview—only this time make a sincere effort to avoid your past mistakes. One way to do this is to ask yourself the following questions:

1. Did you ask for a specific job?

2. Did you review your qualifications clearly and satisfactorily? Did you inspire confidence in your abilities?

3. Did you dress appropriately? Was your personal appearance good?

4. Did you exhibit a sincere interest in your prospective employer by showing some knowledge about the operations and policies of the enterprise in which you are seeking employment?

5. Were you pleasant and courteous with everyone you met?

6. Were you at ease during the interview, or were you nervous and flustered?

7. Did you give the impression of being a "go-giver" as well as a "go-getter?"

8. Did you make the mistake of bringing up questions of wages and working conditions *before* you were offered the job?

9. Did you criticize a former employer?

10. Did you talk too much, and were you too aggressive?

11. Did you flop into a chair and pull out a cigarette?

12. Did the interviewer ask questions you could not answer?

13. Did you fail to discuss some mutual interest you had with the employer?

14. What, specifically, led the interviewer to deny you the job? How can you avoid a second refusal for the same cause? Do you need more training or education? Do you require greater restraint and self-control?

15. Did you find it hard to say what you wanted to say at any time? If so, why? Would memorizing your personal statement help the next time?

16. What would you do differently during your *next* interview?

LISTEN TO SOUND ADVICE

In addition to asking yourself these questions, talk the whole matter over with someone in whom you have confidence. He or she may be able to spot your weak points, as revealed by the interview, and may be able to give you sound advice. And as one who would truly bear Christ, as one who would seek out a career with a Christopher purpose, you should give careful attention to such advice—provided, of course, that it is really sound and constructive.

The more assistance you can get from every quarter, the greater will be your chance for ultimate success in helping to change the world for the better. Though your role may seem small and insignificant, in the sight of God you are important —you count!

This is something to remember every day of your life and put to practical use.

FOR ADDITIONAL READING

CUNNINGHAM, ED, and LEONARD REED. *Your Career.* New York: Simon & Schuster, 1949. P. 72.

DREESE, MITCHELL. *How to Get the Job.* Chicago: Science Research Associates. P. 48.

HUMPHREYS, J. ANTHONY. *Choosing Your Career.* Chicago: Science Research Associates. P. 48.

KUDER, G. FREDERIC, and BLANCHE B. PAULSON. *Discovering Your Real Interests.* Chicago: Science Research Associates. P. 48.

LARISON, RUTH HOOPER. *How to Get and Hold the Job You Want.* New York: Longmans, Green and Co., 1950. Pp. xii + 264.

LYONS, GEORGE J., and HARMON C. MARTIN. *The Seven Keys to Getting and Holding a Job.* New York: Gregg, 1942. Pp. vii + 241.

Mason, R. E. *How to Write Letters That Get Jobs.* Hollywood: The Marcel Rodd Co., 1946. Pp. xiii + 192.

U. S. Department of Labor, Bureau of Labor Statistics. *Occupational Outlook Handbooks (Bulletin 940)* pp. xi + 453. For sale by the Superintendent of Documents, U. S. Government Printing Office, Washington 25, D.C. $1.75.

WHAT YOU CAN DO IN WASHINGTON

1.

Everyone's Responsibility

A young man who works for a brokerage concern in New York told us a real life story concerning himself which illustrates in glaring detail one of the major causes of our trouble in America today; namely, *lack of personal interest in our own government*. While he was a senior at college this young man once applied—in what he described as a "moment of idealism"—for a job in the State Department. Several months later, however, when the State Department phoned to inform him that he had been accepted for a position overseas immediately after graduation, he got "cold feet" and decided to back out. As he put it: "The thought of leaving New York to go to Europe or South America or the Far East scared me to death." He began to make excuses as to why he couldn't accept the offer. His plans had been changed, he told the State Department official on the other end of the line. Besides, he wasn't even sure he would graduate. Even the official's assurance that they had checked and he was practically certain to get his degree failed to persuade him. He turned down the offer and later took a job in a brokerage house.

A short time ago we met him on the street. His opening words were an expression of regret for passing up the opportunity to serve his country. "Now I'll probably be going into the army to fight in Korea or some place else. If only I and a lot of other fellows like me had made a small sacrifice a few years ago and gone into government, we might have been able to do more than a little to prevent the mess we are now in."

It is small wonder that, in contrast to similar apathy on the part of the average citizen, those practicing subversion have made government their objective. In many instances the government was left with no alternative: if the best Americans turned them down, they had no recourse except to take the next best—and the *next best* in many instances turned out to be the *worst possible*. While we were in Washington gathering material on government for this book, a personnel official in the State Department made this revealing statement: *"At no time in the last ten years have enough people even applied for all the rank-and-file jobs that are open in the State Department."*

A similar lack of interest, it should be remembered, had much to do with preparing the way for the Nazis in Germany. A young lady Christopher made this very point to a young man whom she was trying to encourage to be a government worker. Unable to go into this vital field herself, she had appointed herself a "committee of one" to persuade others to do so. The young man to whom she was talking on this occasion had just completed his law studies and had decided to go into private practice. Her suggestion that he go into government, instead, drew this negative response: "Nothing doing! You can't make enough money in government!"

"That isn't the point!" she flashed back. "You're supposed to put in—not only take out. Remember, it's your government as much as it is anybody's. The trouble with you is you want someone else to do the job for you. You want to let 'George' do it. Well, that's the same mistake the Germans made a while back, and 'George' did it, all right—only his name was Adolf!"

The young man is now in the State Department.

In every country where the good, sound-thinking people neglect to staff their own government, they open the door to every undesirable element to "take over." Throughout history, graft and corruption have left their fatal mark on government, though usually a strong, vital, loyal element in government has resisted their inroads. Today there are too few in government service who have any cause beyond themselves. Too many are self-seekers. They are dedicated to no cause beyond self. Their daily work has no high purpose and responsibility. They think of their jobs as being just another way to earn a living. As a result of this neglect, doors are opened in countless ways to those who enter the field of government not to do GOOD but to do EVIL.

SOMETHING NEW HAS BEEN ADDED

Up to twenty-five years ago there was little danger that any sizable force in our country would get into our government and use the established channels of administration and authority to undermine our country. During the last two decades, however, the rise of Communism has brought about a serious problem. It is succeeding to such an extent, and so cleverly, that its cause is even furthered by well-meaning, though misguided, citizens. These latter are contributing to the downfall of their own country because they are so deluded and confused by the half-truths and double-talk of the subversives that they actually defend the undermining processes that are taking place.

OUR THESIS

With regard to government, the Christopher thesis is the same as that for any other vital sphere: *an abundance of good workers makes for a scarcity of bad ones.*

It is our conviction that a large number of workers with high motivation will take up lifelong careers in government once they realize the tremendous opportunity it offers for serving the good of all; once they comprehend that those who claim to have a true love of God and country should be in the forefront, willing to give their all for this important service.

In times of emergency this realization, this comprehension, is abundantly evident. The generous spirit shown by the majority of Americans in a period of national crisis was tersely summed up by an air-force-reserve officer who, upon hearing of hostilities in Korea, wired this brief message to the Pentagon: *"Willing, dependable, and expendable. Say where and when."*

We believe that a sufficient number with similar disposition and purpose can be found to take up the long-range job of running the biggest business in the world today—the federal government of the United States. All parts of government are important, of course—town, city, county, and state. But all of them could be perfect and still the country could collapse if its very heart, federal government, were to become weak through neglect or be undermined by those who aim to destroy our nation.

A relatively small number of devoted, loyal workers might determine the difference between life and death for America. Lenin, who brought the Communist regime to power in Russia, gave testimony to this fact when he was asked what it was that helped the Reds most in achieving their goal. *"The infirmity of our enemies,"* was his prompt reply. *"If there had been in Petrograd in 1917 only a group of a few thousand men who knew what they wanted, we would never have come to power in Russia."*

HIGHEST MOTIVES

Those who would give themselves to the service of all through federal government must be dominated by the highest spiritual and patriotic motives if they would persevere, despite the hard work, long hours, sometimes low pay, heartaches and headaches that may often be their lot. In addition, they will have to be ever on the alert to promote measures that are for the best interests of the country. They will thereby overcome the deteriorating and demoralizing tendencies that handicap good government, regardless of what administration may be in charge.

Among other things, it should be of special interest to every Christopher-minded worker to recognize:

1. That the object of our government must always be to aid the people, not dominate them; i.e., to secure for each citizen his God-given rights and promote the general welfare.

2. That *too much* government may be even more of a threat to human freedom than *too little* government.

3. That nothing should be done by federal government that more properly should be done by state governments. In the same sense, the state should never assume responsibilities that belong to the city or town. The individual citizen, likewise, should not allow the city, state, or federal government to do for him what he can do by himself or through non-governmental groups.

4. That the use of the taxpayers' money is a sacred trust, involving careful expenditures but avoiding any economizing where our country's best interests would be endangered.

5. That loyalty to country takes precedence under all circumstances over what may be of advantage to a political party and that no special privilege or favor be shown any individuals or groups which might react against the best interests of all.

6. That the one place above all others where there should be no room for those of doubtful or questionable loyalty is federal government. Here should prevail at all times the spirit of George Washington's famous order: *"Only Americans on guard tonight."*

To echo the words of Professor Sterling D. Spero of the Graduate Division for Training in Public Service of New York University: *"To disparage the whole problem because so little disloyalty has been found among so many employees is, of course, nonsense. To speak of a little bit of disloyalty is like speaking of a little bit of typhoid fever. In these days of 'Fifth Columns' . . . the problem of disloyalty in the public service is unfortunately real."*

The basic test whereby a person is retained or dropped as a government worker should be something more than a failure to prove he is actually a traitor. Serious harm can be done through stupidity, carelessness, or a spineless attitude toward those bent on treason. As Goethe said: *"It is in the half fools and the half wise that the greater danger lies."*

OUR HERITAGE

We have one of the best forms of government in the world—a government which, from its inception, has concerned itself with the individuality of man, his hunger for freedom, his faith in himself and, more especially, his faith in his Creator, and his desire for the permanent expression of these divinely inspired ideals. The Constitution of the United States, drafted in 1787, still stands as the greatest and most durable framework of government ever devised by man.

But a democracy demands something of those who claim its privileges. A man cannot exercise his individual rights without assuming, at the same time, his individual responsibilities!

A career in federal government will help you to discharge those responsibilities. But whether or not you personally can go into government, remember that it is *your* government. No matter who you are, you can do something to see that it is staffed by the best type of American.

INDIVIDUAL RESPONSIBILITY

The Christopher movement, however, does not propose either to train men and women for government work or to place them in the government field. In keeping with the policy established from the very beginning, our sole function is to point out the need, stress a spiritual motivation, and then leave it to each individual to take as much or as little interest as he or she wishes.

Each is on his or her own. Our aim is to develop in as many persons as possible the concept which a senior at the University of California expressed in these words:

"This is my world just as much as it is anybody's. And I'm going to work just as hard to save it as others are working to wreck it."

In this course on your role in federal government in Washington or in its branches over the nation, therefore, we merely underline the "why" and "wherefore" and leave the rest to each individual to develop in his or her own way.

We are convinced that hundreds of thousands can be found who will dedicate themselves to the cause of good government with the same devotion, loyalty, and enthusiasm that young couples display when they undertake the big responsibility of marrying and raising families, or with which individuals give themselves to the religious life as devoted servants of God and their fellow men.

Small income, unexpected troubles, lack of glamour, and constant discouragements all become secondary when there is a big cause at stake. All obstacles are taken in stride when the big goal is kept in mind.

In short, *purpose makes the difference!*

Right now there are over two million persons in federal government—the largest civilian group of federal employees that has existed in the peacetime history of *any* nation. During the past twenty years federal employment has multiplied over three and one half times. During the same period the federal pay roll has multiplied six times. Yet even with this large increase in personnel and financial outlay, the federal job turnover rate still averages about 2.9 per cent a month.

This means that thousands of vacancies have to be filled each year . . . an impossible task if all appointments were to be filled from Civil Service ranks. The result has been that over fifteen thousand new employees are being appointed each month on a *temporary* basis until such time as an official Civil Service examination can be held.

OUR PURPOSE

Since the object of this course—as of all the others—is merely to "point the way" and re-emphasize the necessity of high purpose and a sense of direction, we will limit ourselves to a bird's-eye view of federal government as centered in Washington, with particular stress on its personnel side.

2.

Departments and Agencies

As you sit in your living room, reading the evening newspaper or listening to the radio, federal government—with all its departments, commissions, and agencies—may often seem beyond the normal circle of your everyday existence. Yet in almost everything you do the effects of federal government can be felt.

Some idea of the far-reaching influence of federal government on the lives of our people may be gained if you would imagine that you are the President of the United States, sitting in your office at the White House. There the whole panorama of government unfolds before you. Cabinet officers, diplomatic officials, legislative and administrative heads, in an almost unending procession, beat a path to your door. The country and the world are at your finger tips.

In a specific way this is possible because of the reports you, as President, will receive regularly from no less than *fifty-two government agencies* and *nine regulatory commissions*.

It is not our function here to go into each of these agencies and commissions in detail. The subject of government is so vast that it would be impossible here to cover it in its entirety. All that *is* possible here is to *list* the agencies and commissions, with the knowledge that a mere glance over them should prove a forceful reminder of the ramifications of our governmental structure. If the President allowed himself an average of one hour a week for each of the sixty-one divisions mentioned above, he would have to devote about nine hours a day for all seven days of the week to that task alone.

For your information, these agencies and commissions are:

STAFF OFFICES

1. National Security Council
2. National Security Resources Board
3. The White House Office
4. Bureau of the Budget

5. Council of Economic Advisers

CABINET DEPARTMENTS

6. Department of State
7. Department of Treasury
8. National Military Establishment
9. Department of the Army
10. Department of the Navy
11. Department of the Air Force
12. Department of Justice
13. Post Office Department
14. Department of the Interior
15. Department of Agriculture
16. Department of Commerce

17. Department of Labor

NON-CABINET AGENCIES

18. Federal Security Agency
19. Federal Works Agency
20. Housing and Home Finance Agency
21. Veterans Administration
22. National Archives
23. Federal Mediation and Conciliation Service
24. Panama Canal
25. Selective Service System
26. National Selective Service Appeal Board
27. Economic Cooperation Administration
28. War Assets Administration
29. Office of the Expediter
30. Philippine Alien Property Administration
31. Office of Defense Transportation
32. Motor Carrier Claims Commission
33. War Claims Commission
34. Philippine War Damage Commission
35. Indian Claims Commission
36. Tax Court of the United States
37. National Mediation Board
38. Atomic Energy Commission
39. Railroad Retirement Board
40. Tariff Commission

41. National Advisory Commission for Aeronautics
42. American Battle Monuments Commission
43. Displaced Persons Commission
44. Tennessee Valley Authority
45. Reconstruction Finance Corporation
46. Federal Deposit Insurance Corporation
47. Export-Import Bank
48. Smithsonian Institution
49. Civil Service Commission
50. National Capitol Park & Planning Commission
51. National Capitol Housing Authority
52. Commission of Fine Arts

PLUS THESE INDEPENDENT REGULATORY COMMISSIONS

1. Securities & Exchange Commission
2. Federal Reserve Board
3. National Labor Relations Board
4. Interstate Commerce Commission
5. Federal Trade Commission
6. Federal Power Commission
7. Federal Communications Commission
8. Civil Aeronautics Board
9. Maritime Commission

ALL IMPORTANT

Needless to say, each division of the federal government listed here should have only loyal, devoted personnel in every position, from the least job in the most obscure department to the most responsible post in the most vital government office—personnel like the man, now high in federal administrative life, who said that he had the philosophy of dedication to public service instilled in him at his mother's knee. "My parents taught me by example, as well," he added. "My dad had to leave school when he was nine, but later on he studied and studied, all on his own, with one purpose in mind: to pass a Civil Service test and become part of government. And eventually he succeeded. The job to which he was finally appointed wasn't high in federal service—only that of a mail carrier—but there wasn't a prouder man in the world than Dad the day

he returned from his first mail route. He was working for the government . . . that's all that mattered. And he used to explain to me and my brothers what a tremendous privilege it was to be part of the greatest government in the world. He said we ought to have more good, God-fearing men and women in government, because they reflected the American people and could mold public opinion and really influence all mankind.

"In later years," this official continued, "when my parents were getting old and I had been abroad on diplomatic service for a long time, I began to think that perhaps I wasn't doing my duty by them . . . that I should be near them in their declining years. So I wrote home to that effect. My dad promptly wrote back telling me to stay where I was. 'It's God's will that you stay there,' he said. 'You have a job to do. There's something more important in life than your parents!' "

OF PARTICULAR CONCERN

Every job in federal service is important. However, there are some sections of government which are more important than others in regard to the security of our country and the well-being of all our citizens.

DEPARTMENT OF STATE. Leading all others in importance, the condition of this department's "health," efficiency, and loyalty can make or break our country—and that is no overstatement. At the same time it can affect the destiny of other countries the world over.

The Secretary of State heads some twenty-two thousand employees. The department proper has about eight thousand men and women, most of whom are stationed in Washington. The Foreign Service—which is responsible to the Secretary of State but which represents all departments and agencies of the government—comprises about fourteen thousand persons. These latter, in turn, staff more than two hundred and eighty embassies, legations, other diplomatic missions, and consular offices maintained by the United States in some seventy-five countries. Through the various offices of the State Department the world, in effect, becomes a stage on which the actors are subject to the directions and assistance of those behind the scenes.

In another section we will discuss the State Department in considerably more detail. We should like to give similar prominence to the other branches of government which we will mention briefly here. However, the limitations of space prevent us from doing so. But even an abbreviated glance at the various departments other than the Department of State should give the Christopher-minded person a fairly good idea of the opportunities and possibilities in the field.

DEPARTMENT OF JUSTICE. The chief purposes of this department are to provide the means for the enforcement of the federal laws, to furnish legal counsel in federal cases, and to interpret the laws under which other departments act. It conducts suits in the Supreme Court in which the United States is concerned, supervises federal penal institutions, and—through the facilities of the Federal Bureau of Investigation (FBI)—investigates and detects violations against federal laws. It represents the government in legal matters generally, rendering legal advice and opinions, upon request, to the President and the heads of executive departments. The Attorney General supervises and directs the activities of the United States district attorneys and marshals in the various judicial districts.

NATIONAL MILITARY ESTABLISHMENT. This division consists of the Office of the Secretary of Defense, the Department of the Army, Department of the Navy, and the Department of the Air Force. Together with these departments are other agencies, such as the Joint Chiefs of Staff, the War Council, the Munitions Board, and the Research and Development Board. Civilian employees of these departments and agencies perform invaluable service in contributing to our national defense and security, especially at this critical period in our history.

DEPARTMENT OF COMMERCE. The statutory functions of the department are to foster, promote, and develop foreign and domestic commerce, the mining, manufacturing, shipping, and fishing industries, and the transportation facilities of the United States.

Other activities include population, agricultural, and other census compilations; collection, analysis, and dissemination of commercial statistics; coastal and geodetic surveys; establishment of commodity weights, measures, and standards; supervision of the issuance of patents and the registration of trade-marks; establishment and maintenance of aids to air navigation, the certification of airmen, the inspection and registration of aircraft; supervision of the issuance of weather forecasts and warnings; development of inland waterways; supervision of the operation of government-owned barge lines; and declassification and dissemination of scientific and technical data.

DEPARTMENT OF LABOR. In addition to other responsibilities, this department is charged with administering and enforcing statutes designed to advance the public interest by promoting the welfare of the wage earners of the United States. This is accomplished by improving their working conditions and advancing their opportunities for profitable employment.

The policies of the department are established by and its work directed by the *Secretary of Labor,* assisted by the Under Secretary and Assistant Secretaries. The general administrative staff consists of the Solicitor, Director of the Office of Budget and Management, Director of Personnel, and the Director of Information. The library, a service unit, maintains library facilities for the entire department.

In addition to the above offices, the department is made up of the following major units: (1) Bureau of Apprenticeship, (2) Office of International Labor Affairs, (3) Bureau of Labor Standards, (4) Bureau of Labor Statistics, (5) Bureau of Veterans Reemployments Rights, (6) Wage and Hour and Public Contracts Division, and (7) Women's Bureau.

DEPARTMENT OF THE INTERIOR. This department is responsible for the major programs in land, water, and mineral resources. Its jurisdiction extends from the islands of the Caribbean to the Arctic Circle and down again to the South

Pacific. It includes the custody of seven hundred and fifty million acres of land, the welfare of two million persons in our territories and island possessions, as well as the guardianship of four hundred thousand Indians and thirty thousand Alaskan natives. Among the many positions where Christopher-minded persons could serve God and country are those on the Program Staff, Divisions of Information, Personnel Supervision, and Management, and Administrative Services.

FEDERAL SECURITY AGENCY. In many ways this is one of the most important branches of federal government. It was established for the purpose of grouping under one administration those agencies of the government whose major functions are to promote—within *reasonable* limits—social and economic security, educational opportunities, and the health of the nation's citizens. Especially vital are the offices of Education, Vocational Rehabilitation, Public Health Service, and Social Security Administration.

Even a casual reading of the above divisions of the Federal Security Agency will give some idea of how much influence it wields over the lives of the American people. In the right hands it can advance the cause of justice and progress. In the wrong hands it can work untold harm. For example, under the jurisdiction of the Agency is the *Children's Bureau*, which puts out booklets for parents on child guidance.

Some time ago a booklet was sent out by this bureau which many considered to contain suggestive pictures, questionable treatment of sexual problems, and justification of moral transgressions. A young Jewish girl in one congressman's office called the matter to the congressman's attention. And he took immediate action. Through his efforts, and others like him, the offending booklet was taken out of circulation. The fact remains, however, that prior to its being withdrawn, considerable damage had already been done.

MOST ARE GOOD

This example is not meant to reflect on the general character of the great majority in federal service. For the most part our government is staffed by honest, loyal, competent men and women. But government is likewise the target of those who would destroy our country and take from us the God-given liberties for which the founders of our nation sacrificed so much. And, in varying degrees, those apostles of evil have been successful.

Because of this, and because the battle lines are being more sharply drawn between those who are for God and those who are against Him, there is not a moment to be lost. Those who are for God and country must make their voices heard, must get into the fields that count—and government is one of them —and work as hard to preserve our free way of life as do those who work to wreck it.

3.

The State Department

Those who aim to "reach for the world" could find no better spot to accomplish this objective than the State Department. As we mentioned in the first section, rank-and-file jobs in this department are often without applicants. The State Department even has *recruiting teams* going around the United States, trying to encourage men and women to take up careers in this highly important division of government.

The jobs which the State Department is seeking to fill are not necessarily those of high authority or responsibility. In State-side departmental service alone almost *half* the eight thousand employees are in lower classifications, such as stenographers, clerks, typists, secretaries, messengers, elevator operators, et cetera. Furthermore—and this is especially important to Christophers who would take up government service as lifetime careers—at least *one third* of the more responsible positions are arrived at by starting in one of the above capacities. *Promotions in the department are made, as a rule, from within.*

For example, consider the case of a fifty-five-year-old career diplomat, at present an ambassador to one of the European countries, who started his government service in 1916 as a postal clerk in Washington.

From that small beginning he progressed to a job as a Foreign Service clerk. Next he transferred to the Treasury Department. Later, after putting himself through college, where he received a law degree in 1928—all this accomplished *after* working hours—he went back into diplomatic service with the State Department. Today he is one of the most highly respected men in Foreign Service and a credit to the country he represents.

Then there is another man who occupies one of the more important administrative posts in our federal government.

This gentleman came to Washington in 1935 with an overpowering desire to work for the Department of State. Jobs were far from plentiful at the time and, while trying to get himself placed, he operated an elevator at the Capitol Building.

Within a short time he managed to secure a job in the Treasury Department in the Division of Procurement. He stayed there for two years—until the division itself was abolished. Then he had to seek employment elsewhere. During the Christmas season he worked as a clerk in a Washington department store. In January he was back at the Capitol, operating an elevator, determined to get back into government.

In August of that same year he succeeded in landing a job in the Department of Labor. Finally, two months later, he realized his long-held ambition: he transferred to the State Department at a salary of two thousand dollars a year. Six months afterward he received his first pay raise, and was promoted successively until, in 1945, he reached the top Civil Service classification. In less than a decade he climbed the government ladder from elevator operator to the high post he now occupies.

In both these cases—and in thousands of others—it was *purpose* that meant the difference between success and failure:

the purpose to work for one of the great countries of the world; the desire to spend a lifetime in devoted, public service.

THE BEST APPROACH

The quickest passport to government service in Washington today is via a Civil Service clerk, stenographer, or typist examination. This applies to men as well as to women. After six months they can be promoted to any job for which they are qualified. To start off with, they could become *junior professional* or *managerial assistants*.

BASIC QUALIFICATIONS

Qualifications for stenographers include an eighty-word-per-minute speed in shorthand and about a forty-five-wpm speed in typing. Stenographers can be appointed immediately, because of the great need for them. After they have received the appointment and are on the job, *they can file for the first Civil Service examination that comes up.*

Within the foreseeable future the State Department will be hiring clerks and stenographers at the rate of more than one hundred per month, with a separation turnover of fifty to seventy-five.

VETERANS' PREFERENCE

On Civil Service examinations veterans get five points extra, over and above the mark they obtain. Disabled vets go right to the top of the list of preference ratings, even if they but barely pass the exams.

Not all vacancies, however, are filled through competitive federal Civil Service examinations, as we have mentioned before. In exceptional cases the State Department may recruit certain types of high-level specialists and technicians possessing such unique qualifications that nation-wide examinations would not be practical. In addition, if, at any time, the Civil Service Commission's list for a particular type of position is exhausted, authority is given to the department to fill such positions on a temporary basis. At the present time nearly all temporary appointments of the latter type are for positions of clerk-stenographer.

BE ON THE ALERT

If you do not have permanent Civil Service status, or if you are not on a current Civil Service list, we suggest that you be on the alert for announcements of Civil Service examinations and take one or more in which you are interested. If you attain an eligibility rating on an examination, your name will be placed on a Civil Service list according to your numerical rating. The Civil Service Commission then refers names, beginning from the top of the list, to fill vacancies in various federal agencies.

Announcements of examinations are posted on the bulletin boards of first- and second-class post offices.

Additional information on specific examinations in which you may be interested is available at your nearest Regional Office of the United States Civil Service Commission.

CONSIDER THESE JOBS

For the Christopher contemplating a career in federal service—the State Department in particular—the following list of positions seems especially important:

Distribution Clerk	Health Counselor
Editorial Clerk	Information Clerk
General Clerk	Intelligence Specialist
Mail, File, and Record Clerk	Information Officer
Research Clerk	Intelligence Research Analyst
Clerk-Stenographer	Labor Economist
Clerk-Typist	Librarian
Code and Cipher Clerk	Library Assistant
Editor	Liaison Officer
Educational Specialist	Management Analyst
Employee Counselor	Messenger
Executive Assistant	Commercial Treaty Specialist
Executive Secretary	Communications Analyst

Communications Officer	Professional Writer
Conference Administration Assistant	Program & Planning Analyst
	Receptionist
Conference Aide	Proofreader
Correspondence Clerk	Recruitment & Placement
Correspondence Reviewer	Officer
Cryptanalyst	Research Assistant
Personnel Clerk	Secretary
Personnel Assistant	Security Officer
Personnel Officer	Shorthand Reporter
Photostat Operator	Stenographer
Placement Assistant	Translator
	Typist

OVER-ALL PICTURE

This job listing is, admittedly, far from complete. In the relatively short space devoted to government it would be impossible for us even to mention *every* important position. Nevertheless, we are trying to give you the over-all picture— the direction in which to head—and then leave it to the initiative of each person to seek out the vital spot where he or she can best make felt his or her influence for good.

INFORMATION CHECK

By law an FBI check is required on all administrative personnel in the higher brackets. In regard to the clerical, typist, and stenographic jobs, the same type of information check is required, except that it is handled by the State Department's own Office of Security. The information is obtained by the department's own investigators. Don't falsify your age or qualifications. Be strictly honest in all you do.

VITAL SERVICE

On the "home front" there is much less shifting of personnel than there is in overseas assignments. But the chance to perform a worth-while, patriotic service to God and country is by no means lacking, even though there may be little color attached to the various jobs.

A man high in government circles told us of working on a special case some time ago that was vital to our country's interest. And he spoke of what it meant to have reliable, sound-thinking assistants in such a time of great stress and urgency. Of one young woman who worked with him on this assignment, he said: "That girl must have averaged sixteen hours a day. In all my life I have never seen such devotion to duty. She did a job that no man could do and enabled me to accomplish a job that I could not possibly have completed successfully without her."

4.

Foreign Service and Key Spots within the Department

WONDERFUL OPPORTUNITIES

In the division of Foreign Service, perhaps more than in any other branch of the State Department, there are wonderful opportunities for young men and young women. College graduates can take clerical jobs—file clerks, accounting clerks, et cetera—and then can advance to small posts in overseas areas. They will be assigned to each post for *two years,* at the end of which time they will be transferred to another spot both for advancement and experience.

On the Foreign Service Exchange Program, now in effect, foreign officers are brought home and the men at home are sent overseas, in order to give each group a well-rounded knowledge of the workings of the Foreign Affairs Division.

For all foreign service there is granted rent and food allowances plus money exchange—these in addition to the prescribed base salary.

INTERN PROGRAM

Also, for those who have graduated from college, or will do so in the near future, the recent announcement by the State Department that it is launching a four-part program to encourage and train young college graduates for future leadership in the Department of State should prove of especial interest. This program has been undertaken with the co-operation of colleges and universities throughout the United States, who handled their own initial screening by setting up Nominating Boards of from three to five members, which will select outstanding and qualified students for participation in the government's program.

This four-part program is divided as follows:

1. An Intern Program which will offer to those who make the grade the opportunity of a permanent appointment to the Department of State.

2. A United Nations Summer Student Intern Program involving special work assignments in Geneva, Switzerland. Under this program foreign students will be offered the opportunity of coming over to this country on an exchange basis.

3. A special Student-Assistant Program which entails an approximate three-month plan, with work assignments assisting departmental officers.

4. Professor and Student Summer Seminar on Foreign Affairs, with special research assignments, lectures, discussions, and observational tours.

KEY SPOTS WITHIN THE STATE DEPARTMENT

One of the key spots within the State Department both in regard to Foreign Service and State-side administration is the *Office of Personnel*.

This office is responsible for the development, execution, and co-ordination of personnel administration and policies for the department, the Foreign Service and special programs administered by the department itself from time to time.

A girl we heard about, an Oklahoman by birth, is a splendid

example of the good that one person can do in such a vital governmental division.

A few years ago, while en route to New York to get, as she puts it, "one of those glamorous jobs I was always reading about in the magazines," she stopped off in Washington to visit her sister who had married and moved there sometime previously. Before she left home her father had told her to get into government, explaining that "they need people like you." The advice hadn't impressed her very much then, for, as she confessed, "Government was the last place I wanted to go."

However, since her father had extracted a promise from her at least to stop by the Civil Service Commission and see what kind of questions they asked—purely for his own information, so he said—she went to make suitable inquiry. Immediately she was sent over to the State Department for an interview. There the woman in charge of personnel told her she was just the girl they wanted to fill a certain position. So she filled out a "57"—a government application blank—and in a short time was on the staff as a typist.

Today she has a most responsible job in the personnel section, where she has had many opportunities to recommend personnel practices and policies that may make government employees more anxious to stay in federal service.

During the war she went overseas to replace a worker who was scheduled to leave on the assignment but who was suddenly taken ill. "I never dreamed that working for the government could be so constructive and so satisfying," she told us. "If I have any regrets, it's just that I didn't get to Washington sooner!"

Inasmuch as there are many phases of personnel work, all somewhat alike in general nature but admitting of certain diversified specializations, the Christopher who has made up his or her mind to take up a lifetime government career might consider the following three subdivisions of personnel administration:

1. *Division of Departmental Personnel.* This section is responsible for the planning, development, and execution of

policies and procedures governing (a) recruitment, placement, transfer, promotion, demotion, and separation of employees of the department; (b) administration and execution of the applicable provisions of the laws and regulations controlling government personnel-management program. This section covers some eight thousand employees.

2. *Division of Foreign Service Personnel.* This section develops and directs an adequate and efficient personnel program for the Foreign Service of the United States. This branch alone covers fourteen thousand persons.

3. *Foreign Service Institute.* This section is responsible for improving the skills, broadening the understanding, and developing the abilities of Foreign Service and departmental personnel and other federal employees who require instruction in the field of foreign relations. It furnishes extensive and systematic training and promotes and fosters programs of study incidental to such training.

OFFICE OF INTELLIGENCE RESEARCH

This office is charged with planning, developing, and implementing an integrated intelligence-research program for the State Department, co-ordinating it with those of other federal agencies. This is done in order to provide the department with foreign intelligence necessary for the formulation and execution of American foreign policy and to provide the Central Intelligence Agency with studies pertinent to the national security. Competence is required, to be sure, in intelligence service, but even more essential are loyalty and devotion to the best interests of the nation. Policymakers must depend on the conscientious efforts of trustworthy individuals way down in the ranks.

OFFICE OF INTERNATIONAL INFORMATION (OII)

The last, but not least, division of the State Department which we have identified among the key spots is the Office of International Information, more commonly known as the OII.

This office is responsible for supporting the foreign policy of the United States by giving the peoples of other countries a true picture of the aims, policies, and institutions of the United States and by promoting mutual understanding between Americans and other nationalities as an essential foundation of durable peace.

It is also responsible for providing appropriate assistance to private activities contributing to this purpose.

DIVISIONS OF OII

The Office of International Information consists of these *three* divisions:

    A. Division of International Press and Publications
    B. Division of International Broadcasting
    C. Division of International Motion Pictures

MAJOR FUNCTIONS

At a time in world history when it is so important that a true picture of what America is and what it stands for should be presented to people of all nations beyond our borders, consideration should be given to the following six major *functions* of OII:

1. It plans and develops, for final approval by the Assistant Secretary for Public Affairs, the international information policies of the department.

2. It develops, co-ordinates policy *for*, and supervises the execution *of* the United States program in the field of international information.

3. Disseminates information abroad about the United States through all appropriate media.

4. Promotes freedom of information.

5. Encourages and assists private agencies in their international information activities; insures the use of private facilities wherever practicable in carrying out the department's international information program.

6. Assists the Assistant Secretary for Public Affairs to discharge his responsibilities in connection with the U. S. Advisory Commission on Information and, on his behalf, insures

departmental leadership of all interdepartmental international information committees.

APPLICATIONS

Persons wishing to apply for positions in the Office of International Information should send applications to: *Division of Departmental Personnel, Department of State, Washington, D.C.* However, those interested solely in the work of the International Broadcasting Division (*Voice of America*) should submit their applications to: *Field Personnel Officer, Department of State, 250 West 57th Street, New York, N.Y.*

The Voice of America is one of the most powerful means of transmitting to the people of other lands the aims, aspirations, and free way of life which we in the United States hold dear. In one recent month some twenty-nine thousand letters were received at the Voice's headquarters, telling what it means to the listeners who wrote them and pleading that the broadcasts continue. The letter writers also asked to be put on the mailing list to receive *The Voice,* a program publication printed in eight languages. This publication now has a permanent mailing list of seven hundred and fifty thousand.

Approximately six hundred and fifty are employed to put the Voice of America on the air. This includes editors, script writers, translators, announcers, clerks, typists, et cetera, many of whom are required to double on jobs—such as translator-announcer, writer-producer, and so on.

QUICK RESULTS

How effective the Voice has become in informing and encouraging those behind the Iron Curtain is evident from one incident which happened not too long ago. The Voice was on the air when Madame Kasenkina made her historic leap from a window of the Soviet Consulate in New York. Immediately the Voice interrupted its program to give the news flash and repeated it at the program's end, with additional information. Within two and one half hours the story was all over Moscow, although it had not been printed in the local press or heard over the Russian radio. General Bedell Smith, our Ambassador, heard the news from a servant who, in turn, had learned of it from a chauffeur. General Smith said later that it was amazing the number of Russian people—clerks, stenographers, laborers, even Soviet guards—who knew all about Madame Kasenkina's jump to freedom.

Since the Voice of America does wield such great influence in expressing the American way, it is recommended as a vital spot to those who wish to take up full-time Christopher careers in government work.

THE TIME IS NOW!

Today, as never before in our history, we need competent, high-minded men and women to dedicate themselves to service in *all* branches of government work.

All government is important—local, county, state, and federal. But, as we pointed out earlier, federal government is the most important. Unless federal government is strong, honest, and efficient, all other phases of governmental life will be seriously affected.

Fortunately we do have many men and women in this influential sphere who are a credit to their country. They stand for honest government based on sound moral principles— principles which the godless would trample in the dust. But thousands more are needed all the time to go into government with a Christopher purpose.

The opportunities are there . . . opportunities which may affect the destiny of all mankind. The only thing lacking is enough zealous, sound-thinking, patriotic Americans who will make government—good government—their personal concern.

There is a challenge to be met, especially in these troubled times. And we believe that, with God's help, it will be. Once enough Christopher-minded persons take up lifetime careers in the vital fields, once enough go into government with the purpose of serving God and country to the best of their ability, then—and then only—will there be great hope for the future.

FOR ADDITIONAL READING

DIVISION OF THE FEDERAL REGISTER, NATIONAL ARCHIVES ESTABLISHMENT. *United States Government Organization Manual,* 1949. Pp. v + 725. For sale by the Superintendent of Documents, U. S. Government Printing Office, Washington 25, D.C. $1.00.

MACMAHON, ARTHUR W., and JOHN D. MILLETT. *Federal Administrators.* New York: Columbia University Press, 1939. Pp. xiv + 524.

McLEAN, JOSEPH E. (ed.) *The Public Service and University Education.* Princeton: Princeton University Press, 1949. Pp. vi + 246.

O'BRIEN, JAMES C., and PHILIP P. MARENBERG. *Your Federal Civil Service.* New York: Funk and Wagnalls, 1940. Pp. xvi + 501.

OGG, FREDERIC A., and P. ORMAN RAY. *Essentials of American Government.* New York: Appleton-Century-Crofts, 1947. Pp. vi + 728.

O'ROURKE, L. J. *Opportunities in Government Employment.* New York: Garden City Publishing Company, 1940. Pp. xii + 307.

PFIFFNER, JOHN M. *Public Administration.* New York: The Ronald Press Co., 1946; Revised ed. Pp. xii + 621.

PLISCHKE, ELMER. *Conduct of American Diplomacy.* New York: D. Van Nostrand Co., 1950. Pp. xiv + 542.

SPERO, STERLING D. *Government Jobs and How to Get Them.* Philadelphia: J. P. Lippincott, 1945. Pp. xviii + 358.

RESHAPING THE FUTURE IN TELEVISION

1.

A Tremendous Power for Good

The tremendously far-reaching effect of the new giant of the communications industry—television—ranks in one sense with the development of atomic energy as having one of the greatest potential impacts on modern civilization—for good or for evil. The line in Shakespeare about all the world being a stage will be put into practical application by the mere twist of a dial. The magic of television will bring into reality what the rubbing of Aladdin's lamp accomplished in the fairy tale. *History will be seen as it is being made.*

Our responsibility to see that this new medium for the millions is used for the betterment of mankind is underlined with great emphasis in the statement of David Sarnoff, Chairman of the Board of the Radio Corporation of America, as quoted in the book, *4000 Years of Television,* by Richard Hubbell.

"Sociologists," says Mr. Sarnoff, "have pointed to the immense potentialities of propaganda in television. The great mass of the human race is often swayed by the appeals to emotion rather than to reason. Millions of people in countries which have succumbed to dictatorships have undergone extraordinary changes in their expressed actions and beliefs.

"These changes have been wrought in a short time, with the

aid of radio propaganda. Vast populations have been led to accept ideologies contrary to their former beliefs because of the skillfully presented ideas which were spread with the speed of light into every home of those unfortunate lands.

"With the advent of television, it has become even more important than before that we preserve our precious right to freedom of discussion—and guard television against exploitation in transmitting propaganda intended to arouse racial animosities, religious hatreds, and destructive class struggles. Television's ultimate contribution can be its role in the betterment of the life of the nation and, at the same time, the greater development of the life of the individual.

"We who have labored in the development of this ultimate form of communications are proud to have the opportunity to aid in the progress of mankind. It is our earnest hope that television will help us to strengthen the United States as a nation of free people and high ideals, in war and in peace."

VASTNESS OF THE FIELD

To give you some idea of the immensity of the whole area of video presentation and programming and its acceptance by the general public, one of the top authorities in the field told us recently that within a few years there will be twenty million television sets in the homes of America! That means an outlay of approximately five billion dollars for the receiving sets alone, not to mention the additional billions of dollars which will be spent on the building of TV stations, offices, studios, et cetera.

All this, of course, is concerned with what might be called the technical aspects which will accompany the growth of television. More important, however, are the *kinds of programs* which are sent into American homes. No matter how perfect television becomes from a physical standpoint, if the highest standards of good, wholesome entertainment and information are not maintained, it will fail to realize its potentialities as one of the greatest forces for *good* ever devised. It can become a potent force for evil.

Television, properly handled, will create a new medium of entertainment, with new types of programs and new art forms never seen before. It will create thousands of new jobs for producers, directors, writers, actors, technicians, and a personnel force trained along the specific lines peculiar to television. It can easily foster a new type of journalism, providing up-to-the-minute news coverage in visual and aural form. In the not-too-distant future TV will encompass the world, bringing to hundreds of millions of people every form of public information, entertainment, and education, exchanging the ideas of one nation for those of many others.

STATISTICS TELL THE STORY

The influence television can have on the American public and the demoralizing effect it can exert if put in the wrong hands is graphically illustrated by a survey which revealed that:

Eighty per cent of TV owners say that children like television better than radio.

Sixty-six per cent say TV keeps children home more.

Ninety-two per cent of TV owners say families get together to watch the same video programs, as compared with only 27 per cent who get together to listen to the same radio programs.

Movie attendance among children in TV homes dropped from 4.7 to 3.1 times per month.

People who have had their sets less than three months spend almost seventeen hours a week watching the various video presentations. Those who have owned sets for two years or more look at TV for about thirteen hours a week—which is still quite a lot of "looking"!

Surveys show that reading generally drops off considerably after a TV set arrives. Children who used to find delight in books now spend those hours in watching cowboy films on a Saturday or Sunday afternoon. And this fact led one radio-television editor to state: *"The reading habit is thus nipped in the bud. It is to be hoped that video, once it grows up enough to realize its heavy responsibilities to the public, tries in some fashion to promote the reading of good books among young and old."*

CAUSE FOR CONCERN

The matter of program content and standards of entertainment poses an urgent problem which requires a prompt and *constructive* solution. That this should be so is apparent to those who have watched television grow to its present position in the all-inclusive area of communications. Only recently a group of citizens on the West Coast sent to the Federal Communications Commission in Washington a set of figures covering one week's programming over six California television stations. During this period they counted:

"Ninety-one murders, seven stage holdups, three kidnapings, ten thefts, four burglaries, two cases of arson, two jail breaks, the murder by explosion of fifteen to twenty people, two suicides, one case of blackmail. Cases of assault and battery too numerous to tabulate. Also cases of attempted murder. Much action takes place in saloons, brawls too numerous to mention, along with drunkenness; crooked judges, crooked sheriffs, crooked juries."

NOT ALL GUILTY

Naturally not all stations or all programs are guilty of having questionable standards of entertainment. Some stations are quite scrupulous in providing the highest type of programs possible; others, however, are not quite so circumspect. The danger to guard against is that of allowing the lowest type of entertainment planning to set the pace for the industry as a whole.

If certain television presentations are not living up to promised standards—and some are *not*—the solution to the problem lies not in merely pointing out the dangers but in taking *positive, constructive action* to provide high-quality programs.

There are, we believe, *three* basic methods of approach needed in order to put this into *everyday* practice.

METHOD NO.

Encourage men and women to go into the field of television themselves. This means alerting thousands of people to develop within themselves a consciousness of the part they, personally, can play in guaranteeing the best type of video presentation that it is humanly possible to achieve. They can be encouraged to take up *active, full-time careers in television itself.*

There are hundreds of diversified jobs in television which can be filled by those who would enter the field with a Christopher purpose . . . jobs from receptionist and script girl on up to program director and production supervisor.

Not everyone, of course, will succeed in making a place for himself in TV, for the very good reason that for every job open at the present time there are a hundred people making application. But the fact still remains that one person's chance is as good as another's—and a Christopher purpose can make all the difference in the world between success and failure.

METHOD NO. 2

Alert those now in television to the power for good they possess. This method of making television what it was meant to be—a tremendously powerful force which can actually change the world for the better—is that of arousing those *already in the field* to the part they can play in bringing mankind closer to Christ.

METHOD NO. 3

Stimulate public interest in the quality of video presentations. This is one of the most effective ways to secure and maintain high-quality TV programs. Those with poor or bad ideas are most alert in attempting to use the power of public opinion to persuade a station or network to offer a particular type of program or to discontinue another type which runs counter to their wishes. This method has proven remarkably successful in the companion field of radio.

That not enough good people realize the power of public opinion, especially when it is expressed in sufficient volume, prompted one observer to make some penetrating observations on the subject. Confining himself to *daytime video* shows in this instance, he pointed out:

"The way I look at it, the low caliber and ... quality of the programs being offered to what the industry refers to as the 'housewife trade' is an insult to the intelligence of the women who comprise the major portion of the daytime audience. But when only hundreds, instead of thousands, take the trouble to protest, then perhaps the daytime listener is getting no better than he or she deserves. ... Think it over!"

If enough people with Christopher purpose think it over, and do more; if they make television their personal concern in any of the three methods mentioned, they can help usher in an era of real peace.

2.

There's a Job in TV for You

One can never tell what effect a few words spoken at the right time may have in guiding men and women into one of the vital fields. Sometimes the most unlikely people will turn out to be the likeliest workers with a Christopher purpose.

Some time ago a group of students at Wellesley College asked me to address them on the Christopher movement. During the talk I told them: "I don't know what your background is, or your faith. To be sure, I wish that you girls would believe all that I hold sacred and essential. But if you believe only one truth of Christ, do something to bring it into the market place." And I continued: "Once you graduate, your big temptation will be to withdraw into your own little worlds and let the big world outside go to the devil. Please don't do that. You are needed, every one of you. If you take a job, try to take one that counts. You, whoever you are, can do something to make the world a bit better for your being in it."

STORY OF ACHIEVEMENT

About six months after this talk, one of the group contacted me and unfolded a simple yet fascinating story of achievement. The young lady said she belonged to no church and had been groping in the dark until she heard the challenge of the Christopher idea. Apparently it hit home with such force that, for the first time in her life, she confessed that she felt it within her power to do something for the good of mankind.

After analyzing the various vital fields, she came to the conclusion that *television* offered the greatest "potential" for accomplishing good. She left her home in New England and came to New York. After considerable difficulty she secured a job in one of the studios—*as a messenger carrying scripts!* The lowly beginning, however, didn't discourage her. She had a purpose, and people with purpose—whether for good or bad—show imagination. They are alert and observant; they know where they are going. This young lady's objective was to get into the heart of television with the motive of doing good. She saw the job of messenger girl as a steppingstone to her goal. Fifteen months later she had become the youngest television producer in the world!

Television is "wide open" for people with creative ideas, for those who are sparked with imagination, initiative, and resourcefulness. But it will take hard work and diligent practice on their part if they are to exert as great an influence on this new medium as do those who have no ideals or whose only purpose is to debase civilization.

THE NECESSARY "INGREDIENT"

Norman Blackburn, a veteran of the radio industry and a key figure in today's expanding television scene, states: *"In my opinion, the most important single requirement for a successful career in television is the same ingredient needed for a successful career in any business—ambition! It is the desire to accomplish a goal. The will to succeed should be the most important thing in your mind—and if this will is strong enough, you will be a success in practically any chosen field of endeavor."*

From a material standpoint, everything that Mr. Blackburn says is only too true. But since the things of this world are fleeting *and those of God are not,* the Christopher-minded person contemplating a career in television will have more than personal ambition and desire for monetary or professional gain to stimulate him. He will go into television not for what he can get out of it but for what he can *put into* it. His objective—like the objective of every Christopher—will be to restore all things in Christ. He will seek to "change the world" for the better by helping to make television what it was meant to be: a power for good which God intends to be used for the benefit of all mankind.

Specifically, he will have these *three* qualities:

1. The desire to enrich the lives of his fellow men with the best type of entertainment and information.

2. Persistence—the urge to keep going, in spite of all obstacles, until a job is completed.

3. A "divine dissatisfaction" with his own efforts, no matter how well done the task or how well accepted by others.

IMPORTANT TO REMEMBER

Unlike the motion pictures and the radio, which have had such a profound effect on the world for the past several decades, television has been kept in the laboratory until almost full grown.

The limitations of radio, where the living voice interprets to the listener what is taking place in a studio, auditorium, or on a football field, are not present in the medium of television. Neither is the limitation of motion pictures, where the visual attraction must, of necessity, suffer a time lag in presentation between the actual filming of an event and its showing to the general public; e.g., newsreels.

The diversity of special talents which television demands of those actively engaged in the field are numerous indeed. To give you an idea of what we mean, consider the Fred Waring Show on TV. This particular program has probably the largest behind-the-scenes organization in the entire field.

While some sixty-five entertainers perform *before* the cameras for the video presentation, there are *ninety-four persons* in action in various capacities *behind* it. There are fourteen stagehands, four cameramen, two camera prop men, four men at the camera controls, four sound men, two sound boom men, a four-man lighting crew, four stage managers, four directors, three commercial writers, five commercial prop workers, sixteen ushers, three house managers, two advertisement-agency contact men, seven publicity men, two business representatives, two writers, two script girls, one ticket girl, one producer, five musical arrangers, one dance arranger, two music librarians, one attorney, and a chef!

Of all these job categories, probably the greatest shortage of competent, sound-thinking men and women exists in the *writing* branch of television. According to Maxine Keith, lecturer on TV at New York University, City College of New York, and McGill University, Montreal, Canada, there is a *"screaming scarcity"* of imaginative television writers. This is not mentioned by way of disparagement to those already in the field. Obviously, since television is a new medium, it requires a new writing technique which will take into consideration the fact—as was pointed out before—that TV embraces the aural effects of radio and the visual effects of motion pictures and combines the two with the sense of *immediacy*—the portrayal of an event as it is actually taking place.

BE PREPARED

No matter what job you aim for, however, if your Christopher purpose is sincere you should be prepared to *start at the bottom of the TV ladder if necessary,* and then go on to profit by your experiences.

This is a point we cannot emphasize too strongly. As a

personnel director in one of the larger networks stated so well: *"Whatever your ultimate aim in radio or television, when you apply for a network position come prepared with skills and abilities that radio and television can use. And come prepared, too, for the fact that you have to start in the lower ranks. Our openings do not come in the top-job bracket or even in intermediate jobs. We promote to those positions. Year after year our most frequent openings for men are in page, messenger, and junior-clerk jobs. The most frequent openings for women are for clerk-typists and secretaries. From such beginning jobs you can progress, as many of our employees have done, to the more specialized and more interesting assignments.*

"Be sure to seize every opportunity to view television programs. Watch at a friend's house, club, public place—anywhere you can gain access to a set. Familiarity with many of the programs will provide a basis for more understanding and intelligent application in your interview for any job in the field."

This personnel director went on to explain that some employees who started with the company as messengers, office clerks, and pages now hold such positions as assistant night program manager, news writer, press writer, production director, script writer, senior program clerk, station contact representative, studio manager, and writer-announcer.

Employees who started as stenographers and secretaries now include: administrative assistant, employment manager, executive officers' secretaries, junior press writer, office manager, playreader and script editors.

David Sarnoff, head of RCA, started in radio as a junior telegraph operator. Niles Trammell, Chairman of the Board of NBC, started as a salesman. The director of research started as a statistician. The assistant to the vice-president of one of NBC's largest departments began as a secretarial assistant. A senior script writer started as a typist. Two senior announcers started as pages. The manager of audience promotion began as a stenographer-clerk.

Frank Stanton, president of the Columbia Broadcasting System, started in that network's research department in 1935. G. Richard Swift, general manager of WCBS in New York, hired out as an apprentice (better known as an office boy) just sixteen years ago. In 1934 Arthur Hull Hayes became a salesman for CBS. He is now vice-president in charge of the network's San Francisco office.

KEEP IT IN MIND

There is a place for *you* in television, then, provided you have the perseverance, the resourcefulness, the ability, and the Christopher purpose. Even if you have only *one talent*, develop that talent to its utmost. Clever, original routines and unique methods of presentation, from a creative standpoint, spell the difference between an amateur and a professional, between a mediocre professional and a good one, between a good professional and a great one. Furthermore, both in a creative and technical sense, the ability to make your own opportunities will prove to be one of the greatest advantages you possess.

3.

"Getting In"

A man now outstanding in the radio-television field recently went on record with this pertinent piece of advice: *"When I was in radio years ago, I was called upon to counsel many young people who had a desire to get in the broadcasting business. I told them to get as close to it as possible, even if this meant working in the parking lot next door to the broadcasting station. There, at least, their daily contacts would be with those people in whose careers they were most interested. I can offer the same suggestion to those who contemplate a career in television. Pretty much the same technique could easily and profitably be applied."*

A young man from Buffalo is an outstanding example of the

effectiveness of this approach. Some years ago he came to New York, determined to get into the communications field because he saw in it a chance to exert his influence for good. He first job was with a large magazine. It wasn't a very high-paying job, but it was a start—and he proceeded to make the most of it. As time went on, and as he was advanced to more responsible positions, he studied writing and methods of production—all with an eye to putting them to future use. When television began to develop he decided to "get in on the ground floor" as soon as he could. The change-over, though it involved a considerable reduction in salary at the beginning, didn't stop him. He had a sincere Christopher purpose—and that purpose made all the difference in the world. Today he has some thirty-five writers and directors under his supervision and is responsible for several of the most outstanding shows on TV.

CHANGE WITH THE TIMES

Because television as a medium of communication, entertainment, and education is still in its formative stages—and is going to be for a few years to come—it follows that the methods, techniques, ideas, values, and concepts of television will undergo many progressive changes before they assume a final pattern, before the unknown and the untried are no longer predominant factors of operation. To be in television when that time comes, to be in a spot where you can make your influence for good felt, will require that you be the type of person who is determined to adapt the changeless truths to our changing times. Throughout the years, while television is growing up, you will have to grow with it. You will have to leave yourself wide open to new ideas, new methods, new suggestions, while at the same time never compromising your basic principles.

BE SPECIFIC

When you apply for a job in television—and this point has been emphasized by almost every person of authority in the field to whom we have talked—*apply for a specific job*. Too many applicants leave all the work of job selection to the network or station to which they are applying, frequently with discouraging results. Their attitude can best be expressed by the remark: *"Anything you have open will do."*

"Finding out exactly what they CAN do is the big problem for us," one radio-television personnel man confided. *"We're interested in the people who know what they want to do and who have the qualifications to back up their desires. You can take it from me that they'll get every chance to prove their worth."*

YOUR RÉSUMÉ

It is advisable that you prepare a résumé for your prospective TV employer. You should prepare it with the greatest care, for two reasons: (1) it may be a help to your potential employer; (2) it will be a great help to you in evaluating and placing in correct perspective the highlights of your training and experience.

Remember, your résumé is your only personal representative before and after your interview. Be specific regarding all statements of your past achievements. Give dates, facts, figures, places. Make your résumé stand out!

JOB ANALYSIS

Generally speaking, jobs in television can be divided into *six* different categories:

1. Writers and editors.

2. Directors, assistant directors, producers, production assistants, and script girls.

3. Secretaries, stenographers, receptionists, and page boys.

4. Painters, designers, production managers, stage managers, stagehands.

5. Salesmen, publicity men, administrators, research specialists, and psychologists.

6. Engineers, technicians, physicists, chemists, construction experts.

All of these job categories are important. From a Christopher standpoint, however, the "behind-the-scenes" group is the most likely to exert the greatest influence. This group comprises the writers, researchers, directors, producers, secretaries, administrative assistants, and so on.

A WORD OF EXPLANATION

In regard to the field at large, some brief mention should be made here of the functions performed by the various departments of a station or network.

"Programming" employees exercise regulatory and advisory control of commercial programs and completely produce sustaining shows. They develop and contract for new talent, including announcers, producers, news writers, playreaders, script writers, sound-effects men, and music specialists.

The business-management section embraces the financial, legal, personnel, and office-service operations.

The marketing and public-relations branch covers the salesmen who sell time on a station or network's facilities. Also included are the writers and artists who prepare *advertising* and provide publicity to the press on programs, personalities, and company activities; the researchers who compile and interpret statistics of program popularity; and the station-relations representatives who serve as liaison between affiliated stations and/or the network in question.

The technical division includes the engineers, sound and camera men, and so on.

JOB ANALYSIS IN DETAIL[1]

CONTINUITY TYPIST. Types stencils and ditto sheets. Copies continuity and script. Checks continuity stencils and paper jobs for errors in typing, spelling, punctuation. *Qualifications:*

[1]The accompanying analysis has been screened from the National Broadcasting Company's *Job Inventory.* Only those jobs which we feel can be filled to Christopher purpose have been listed in detail.

High-school diploma. Skilled typing. Some experience preferred.

MESSENGER. Sorts and distributes all incoming and outgoing post-office mail. Performs messenger service for both inside and outside errands and for the delivering of interoffice correspondence. *Qualifications:* High-school diploma. Some experience helpful.

SECRETARY. Works in secretarial loan group consisting of three to five members who perform secretarial duties for various departments requiring temporary assistance. Is transferred as secretary to other departments in the company as rapidly as openings occur. *Qualifications:* High-school diploma. Some college or secretarial-school training. Some experience preferred.

EMPLOYER SERVICES ASSISTANT. Plans and organizes employee activities. Edits employee house organ. Conducts personal counseling interviews with employees. *Qualifications:* College degree. Two years' experience in personnel field.

INTERVIEWER. Recruits, interviews, and recommends to departments all staff personnel. Arranges for transfers, promotions, and guidance of employees. *Qualifications:* College degree. Major in personnel administration preferred. Two years' experience in personnel field.

JOB ANALYST. Analyzes job duties. Evaluates jobs and recommends salary ranges. Makes salary-comparison studies and recommendations. *Qualifications:* College degree. Two years' experience in personnel field.

COPY WRITER. Writes copy for newspaper and magazine ads, direct-mail pieces, and commercial copy for broadcast purposes. Originates advertising ideas. *Qualifications:* College degree preferred. Three to five years' copy writing in radio or related field.

GUIDE. Takes visitors on the network radio and television tours. *Qualifications:* High-school diploma.

PAGE. Meets and greets guests at all broadcasts. Collects tickets and sees that audience is seated comfortably in the studio before the broadcast begins. Directs guests to the elevators when program is off the air. Acts as studio receptionist. *Qualifications:* High-school diploma.

CORRESPONDENT. Replies to mail and phone inquiries from other organizations and from the public regarding network programs, artists, and general company activity. Does the research necessary to provide full answers. *Qualifications:* High-school diploma. One year's business experience. College preferred.

MAIL ANALYST. Reads and sorts mail received in division and arranges for proper handling. Answers general telephone inquiries. *Qualifications:* High-school diploma. One year's business experience.

PRESS WRITER. Writes publicity releases on programs, personalities, and company activities for use in newspapers, trade journals, magazines. Arranges for publication of releases. *Qualifications:* College degree or the equivalent in training and experience. Broad cultural background. Three to five years' experience in publicity field.

LIBRARIAN. Manages and develops the network General Library. Reviews all material received. Interviews people who wish special research projects undertaken. Compiles special bibliographies on various subjects related to radio. *Qualifications:* College degree and special library training. Broad cultural background. Two years' experience.

PROGRAM ANALYST. Analyzes network radio and television programs for the purpose of obtaining a historical record of material and personnel used on programs. Compiles special reports from these records. *Qualifications:* College degree preferred. Typing. Broad cultural background. One year's experience in general business field.

SECRETARY. Takes business dictation. Types and files requests for sales-promotion material. Contacts advertising agencies and clients. Quotes rates. Answers telephone. Acts as general assistant in the absence of salesmen. *Qualifications:* High-school diploma. Some college or secretarial-school training. One year's experience in secretarial field.

STATION REPRESENTATIVE. Acts as liaison between affiliated

stations and the network. Through personal visits to the stations and by mail provides information and assistance to station management on the co-ordination of station and network facilities and programs. Provides advice on matters pertaining to the engineering, programming, sales, and business-management phases of broadcasting. *Qualifications:* College. Broad cultural background. Three to five years' experience in radio administration, either network or local.

ANNOUNCER. Announces news, commercial copy, introduction to musical programs, time signals, station identification, et cetera. Acts as master of ceremonies when necessary. *Qualifications:* College. Broad cultural background. Five years' experience as an announcer.

JUNIOR PROGRAM ASSISTANT. Using library services, procures and clears music for studio and film shows. Does music research in connection with program building. *Qualifications:* College. Music specialization. Two to three years' music-program-building experience.

COPY CLERK. Distributes news copy from teletype machines and routes to news desk. Files news scripts and reports. Notifies department of special news features and bulletins. *Qualifications:* High-school diploma. Some office experience.

NEWS WRITER. Writes, rewrites, and/or edits news programs. Determines content and make-up of news broadcasts. *Qualifications:* College degree preferred. Five to ten years' experience in newspaper writing and editing.

PRODUCER DIRECTOR. Assures that scripts for his programs have been cleared, approved, and are ready for rehearsal. Engages cast and arranges time and assures that clearance is complete. Decides upon the sets and props required and the methods by which he can make fullest use of these facilities. Co-operates with the technical director to insure that program requirements are technically possible and that the presentation will be technically perfect. Rehearses cast, perfects presentation, and directs the on-the-air program. *Qualifications:* College. Drama specialization. Broad cultural background. Eight to ten years' experience in radio, motion-picture, or theater production.

PROGRAMMING ASSISTANT. Assures that cast and studio personnel know the dates and time of rehearsals. Arranges for the necessary copies of scripts to be on hand. Assists the studio director or field program director in giving cues and directions and in carrying out other staging requirements of the program. *Qualifications:* College. Drama specialization. Two years' experience in radio, theater, or motion-picture industry.

CASTING DIRECTOR. Interviews and auditions talent. Evaluates qualifications. Maintains and develops classified files of talent, according to background, professional experience, types of roles for which suited. In co-operation with producer-director, selects talent for specific programs. Maintains talent-cost records. *Qualifications:* College. Drama and/or music specialization. Three to five years' casting and program experience.

PLAY EDITOR. Reads and evaluates scripts and program ideas. Works with writers to develop talent for television. Purchases scripts. Assigns adapting and writing. Arranges for library clearance on work to be broadcast. *Qualifications:* College. Drama and/or literature specialization. Two to five years' experience in playreading or publications.

PRODUCTION FACILITIES CO-ORDINATOR. Acts as liaison between producer and technical groups with regard to the creation, construction, transfer, assembly, and placement of props, scenery, and stage material. *Qualifications:* College. Drama specialization. Three to five years' experience in theater work.

FILM LIBRARIAN. Catalogues and maintains file of motion-picture footage owned by network. Stores this film systematically to expedite obtaining particular scenes as required. Maintains a complete index system of individual scenes within the stories. Supplies motion-picture footage of any requested scene. *Qualifications:* High-school diploma. Five years' film-library experience.

FILM EDITOR. Selects films used in television programs. Edits film. Supervises writing of continuity for film. Selects film for stock or atmospheric shots. Processes film. *Qualifications:* College preferred. Three to five years' experience in film industry.

PUBLIC AFFAIRS DIRECTOR. Originates, plans, and, in conjunction with the Program Department staff, supervises programs of an educational, cultural, and religious nature for radio and television. Acts as network public-relations specialist with organizations in these fields. *Qualifications:* Highly specialized experience in educational and related professional fields.

SECRETARY. Performs secretarial duties for public affairs director. Answers mail and assembles preliminary material for programs. Handles occasional research projects. *Qualifications:* College. One or two years' secretarial experience.

PLAYREADER. Reads scripts and considers program ideas submitted by the general public and free-lance writers. Rejects or recommends them to the head of the Script Division. *Qualifications:* College degree preferred. Two years' literary experience, i.e., as assistant to writer, literary-agency work, playreading for theater or motion-picture company.

SCRIPT CLERK. Orders mimeographing and routing of copies of all scripts for scheduled programs in time for rehearsals. Makes up announcers' and producers' Master Book. *Qualifications:* High-school diploma. Typing.

SCRIPT WRITER. Writes scripts for dramatic and variety shows. Writes continuity for musical shows. Writes scripts for auditions, station breaks, and other announcements. *Qualifications:* Some college. Broad cultural background. Three to five years' free-lance, station, or advertising-agency experience in radio-script writing.

Most of the large networks have training programs to help their employees advance. Each year, also, a limited number of employees of potential executive caliber participate in a program of lectures and discussions designed to help them become outstanding candidates for promotion.

READ AND STUDY

To fit yourself further for promotion—or to familiarize yourself with the field if you are not already employed there—it is suggested that you read all available books and trade magazines on television. If possible, attend a good radio-television school. While a diploma from such a school will seldom assure you immediate employment, it will be proof of your familiarity with some of the formats and techniques. And when you do "get your foot in the door" you will not be a complete stranger to your surroundings. Many of the larger colleges and universities have such courses, some taught by network officials. Northwestern and Fordham universities have their own radio stations which give students practical "on the job" experience. Television Workshop in New York is earning a reputation as one of the best schools of its kind.

But don't forget: these schools still will not open the doors for you. They will simply prepare you to do a better job after you gain a place in the radio-television field.

FOUR MAJOR POINTS OF ENTRY

Summarized briefly, there are *four* main points of entry into the radio-television field. They are:

1. Radio-television broadcasting stations (national or local).
2. The radio-television department of an advertising agency.
3. The office of an independent producer.
4. Sound-recording companies which do many of radio-TV commercials.

REMEMBER THIS

There are a great many people anxious to get jobs in television—so many, in fact, that filling these jobs has become a matter of extremely careful selection. But you can try just as hard as anyone else. The field is wide open for men and women with talent, initiative, and *purpose* . . . purpose, most of all.

4.

Writing for Television

A former script-department head of one of the larger networks volunteered to us this information on writing:

"You can learn technique, as most people in radio have learned, through observation and imitation. Listen to and watch TV programs as much as possible. Become as familiar with the actual conditions of telecasting as circumstances permit. Then when you actually sit down to write, you will have a pretty good idea of the field at which you're aiming. When you're away from the typewriter, on the street, in the subway, in department and grocery stores, listen to people talk. Make notes. Make a nuisance of yourself if you have to—but learn actual dialogue! The difference between a good script and a bad one is often the difference between paying close attention to real life and ignoring it!

"Finally, concentrate your 'fire.' Write for one particular program. What you put down on paper has to fit the requirements which one production—no more—makes of its scripters. If you've got the stuff, and if you follow these suggestions which have borne the test of time, I don't see how you can miss."

ADDED REMINDER

As a footnote to what this top authority in the radio-television field had to say, the director of a well-known radio show which has an audience of millions added his own thoughts on the subject. While he confined himself to the radio field, what he said applies equally well to television. Pointing out that the demand for worth-while scripts is increasing, he emphasized the two extremes to be avoided when writing for a show. Many writers, he said, are either too "preachy" and pious or too "naturalistic," too prone to stress the material at the expense of the spiritual. He suggested that writers in general be trained all over again, with these objects in mind:

1. That writing should deal with *principle,* not convention.
2. That writing should spring from *conviction,* not sentiment.
3. That writing should be *positive,* not negative.
4. That writing should be based on *sound, fundamental values.*

WRITING IS HARD WORK

If you wish to write for television, you will require the genuine urge, ability, and purpose that successful writing in any form demands. Write and keep writing. But remember that practice alone, without any incentive, any goal, can tend to make you careless. Therefore, write every script with the idea that you are writing with a *purpose.* Build every situation and polish every speech as if they were your one and only bid for attention.

Script writers engage in a wide variety of writing tasks, including assignments to prepare serials, plays, publicity articles, announcements for musical shows, dramatic works for educational programs, and newscasts. Special courses in radio-television script writing are given in a number of colleges and universities. These courses are valuable in acquainting students with the specific technique of continuity presentation.

Good writing has the best chance of being sold. That point cannot be stressed too often, since one of the major difficulties confronting television today is lack of top-quality programs—which means a lack of top-quality writers to fashion the scripts. To a careless student of human nature this emphasis on the need to raise the standard of entertainment may seem strange, since the very novelty of TV might ordinarily be thought sufficient to hold the viewer's attention. Certainly people look at television programs once or twice for the sheer newness of it. *But beyond that they have to be genuinely entertained.*

Here is the golden opportunity for writers with Christopher purpose to furnish the material for programs of sound, wholesome values which the public is demanding and which, in truth, it has every right to expect. Also, the writing of such worth-while programs is the best possible way of getting worth-while concepts across to the general public.

THE ECONOMIC FACTOR

As should be apparent, not every writer meets with instant success. In many cases the path is a long, hard one, with one discouragement after another rising up to test a person's determination and courage. If you should happen to fall within the group which finds the going difficult, you should have some source of income other than the writing profession. Many well-known radio and television writers, in fact, wrote their first scripts for the free-lance market while they were engaged in some occupation completely removed from the communications field. Once they penned four or five acceptable scripts, of course, they were regarded as professionals and treated as such. But prior to that time they had an *outside source* which provided their livelihood.

If you follow the same procedure while free-lancing, you will have taken the first precaution against possible failure. Moreover, you will have laid the groundwork for a lifetime occupation where your influence as a Christopher can be felt by millions!

STEPS UP THE LADDER

Not all writers, obviously, reach the point where they are *solely responsible* for penning video shows. This does not mean, however, that you cannot earn a living in the television field. It is quite possible that you may be able to work for a well-known TV writer, providing dialogue, developing plot situations, et cetera.

Then, too, you may secure a position on the staff of a program-packaging concern. These are organizations which confine themselves *exclusively* to the building of complete programs, which they, in turn, sell to advertising agencies or to networks directly as a "package." Some program-packaging firms have very elaborate establishments; others less so. But all, as a rule, have a "stable" of good writers to produce package shows—that is, shows complete down to the last detail and ready for production. Frequently, newcomers of proven ability are given the opportunity to help in readying such shows, or they may be hired as apprentice or junior writers by a station or network. In this connection, incidentally, the Radio Writers Guild has specified that 20 per cent of the total number of staff writers may be juniors. Undoubtedly the same provision will apply to TV writers in the not-too-distant future.

A WISE ALTERNATIVE

Assuming, for the sake of argument, that despite careful preparation and the possession of a reasonable degree of talent and creative ability you still are unable to gain entrance to the larger TV stations or networks, *you should try to win a foothold in a smaller station,* where the requirements are not so rigid as elsewhere and where you can get the all-around kind of experience which is so necessary to a full-time Christopher career in television. Since every owner of a radio or television station, big or little, promises to operate in the "public interest, convenience, and necessity," your passport to a TV career may well turn out to be a *service to the community* far greater than you think possible. Especially will this be so if you are motivated with a Christopher purpose, with a desire to change the world for the better.

FINAL COMMENT

Throughout this whole discussion we have tried, purposely, to stress not only the importance of television but the important role you, as an individual, can play in seeing that this vital new medium of communications is used for the betterment of mankind. As one authority in the field observed so well:

"I regard television as the greatest communication force that

has ever been developed. But . . . it's only an instrument. The important thing is what you do with this instrument. The scientific achievement doesn't mean a thing unless our programs, our shows, contribute something to our knowledge, our understanding, our wisdom, our entertainment, and our lives."

Much of the truth in this observation undoubtedly could have been applied to the *radio industry* a quarter century ago, just as it is applicable to television today. From the development of radio, furthermore, we can learn much that will be of value to us in considering a career in TV: types of programs which have proved popular and of sound, lasting influence, audience selectivity, specific demands on the creativeness of those in the communications field, and so on. And it might be well to interject here the thought that radio, despite the rise of television, will continue to make a tremendous impact on American life for some time to come. There are still millions of families in this country who rely on radio for much of their entertainment, information, and education; and while television will be the new giant in the communications industry, radio (and motion pictures also) will continue to have a vital role to play in the life of our nation. This being so, radio should by no means be overlooked by the young man or woman who contemplates a writing career. There are still opportunities to work with a Christopher purpose.

PERSONAL POWER

In regard to television and your responsibility to see that it fulfills the dreams of those who developed it, the more you move among people with a Christopher purpose, the more inspiration, warmth, and compassion will characterize whatever you do, whatever you write. You will be convinced at least of the potential dignity of every man, of a lingering nobility even in the lowliest of humanity. If you have a consuming love for *all* men and not just a *few,* if you write for *everyone* and not just for *some,* you will find yourself stretching to the measure of Christ's sympathy and affection for the whole of mankind.

And whether your aim is to get into television as a secretary or a script writer, as an assistant director or administrator, don't let difficulties or obstacles alter your goal.

Remember, there may be a place in television for you—if you have the perseverance, determination, and Christlike purpose. Remember, too: "Quitters never win. Winners never quit!" Christophers should cherish that motto. They should make it their special slogan in taking up lifetime careers in television—the new giant in the communications industry.

FOR ADDITIONAL READING

ALLAN, DOUG. *How to Write for Television*. New York: E. P. Dutton.

DUPUY, JUDY. *Television Show Business*. Schenectady, New York: General Electric Company.

HUBBELL, RICHARD. *Television Programming and Production*. New York: Murray Hill Books, Inc.

HUTCHINSON, T. H. *Here Is Television*. New York: Hastings House.

HYLANDER, C. J., and HARDING, ROBERT. *An Introduction to Television*. New York: Macmillan.

SOUTHWELL, JOHN. *Getting a Job in Television*. New York: McGraw-Hill.

MAKING ATOMIC ENERGY
A BLESSING

1.

The Possibilities Are Tremendous

In Deming, Washington, a town of three hundred people set in a farming community twelve miles south of the Canadian border, there is a tall, gray-haired science teacher of such unusual ability and devotion to her work that one official, high in the atomic-energy field, was moved to remark: *"If there was one Dorothy Massie in every city and town of the country, the peacetime development of atomic energy as a positive force for good would be assured."*

Miss Massie, who has been a teacher for thirty-one years, the past fourteen at Mount Baker High School where she now instructs, sums up her motivation in these words: "I love science and I love to work with young people. All you have to do to teach boys and girls is bait their interest and give them something to do. Then they'll perform wonders!"

As proof of the accuracy of her opinion, she can point to several of her students whom she has encouraged to enter the Westinghouse Science Talent Search—with exceptionally fine results. One such student, Bill Gunter, won a top Talent Search award just recently, including a four-year science scholarship to Stanford University. One of her girl pupils, Hilda Handel-und, won honorable mention in the Westinghouse competition a few years ago. Another student, Clayton Bentley, aged seventeen, is now working at the Hanford Atomic Project and is expected to go far in the science field. Other pupils of hers came to the attention of atomic-energy officials not long ago on a field trip to the Plutonium Laboratories at the town of Richmond, Washington. There the exhibits her students had prepared under her direction so amazed the onlookers that pictures were taken and a news release was sent out over the various national wire services.

TREMENDOUS INTEREST

Practically every phase of the scientific field interests Miss Massie. For three summers she worked in a local pulp mill as a chemist, just to increase her knowledge. When World War II broke out, she boned up on aeronautics in order better to teach her air-minded youngsters. Later she worked in a radio station in Bellingham, a town sixteen miles distant, where she is a member of the First Baptist Church. Out of the experience gained, she guided her class in the building of a superheterodyne radio set with both long and short waves.

Another example of her initiative and resourcefulness occurred when she assembled one hundred mousetraps and rigged them to shoot pennies in every direction as the catches were released—all this to illustrate chain reaction in atomic energy. She has devised many practical atomic-energy toys—teaching aids for demonstration purposes to her students—upon which various toy manufacturers have urged her to capitalize. But she steadfastly refuses to do so. She doesn't want the money. She just wants to teach. *"There's nothing as exciting as teaching,"* she says, and the crowded classroom, filled with students from various parts of the state, bears testimony to the way in which her enthusiasm has communicated itself to her pupils. Eugene Seaton, one of her youngsters, summed up the reaction to her approach perhaps better than anyone else. *"She teaches you to use your head,"* he said.

During her career Miss Massie could have had other, more

highly paid positions, yet she never took them. Her purpose, of which any Christopher could well be proud, keeps her ever conscious of the tremendous power for good she has in her hands through the teaching of science, particularly as regards atomic energy. She is well aware that this force, which comes from God, can be used for constructive use as well as for defense and can be harnessed for the development of medicine, agriculture, and industry, thus enriching the lives of all mankind. In her own way she has accomplished the objectives the Christophers aim to achieve: (1) she has acted as a "committee of one" to encourage young people to go into this vital field; (2) she has actually *succeeded* in getting some to enter; and (3) she has sparked with a new purpose those already in atomic energy.

A NEEDED EXPLANATION

Very few people know the exact meaning of "splitting the atom." All realize that a terrific force has been discovered. But just what or how still remains vague. In fact, this very ignorance of what atomic energy is tends to create an air of uncertainty, even fear, which would not enter into the picture at all were people to understand the tremendous power for good that God has placed in the hands of man.

Listen to what Dr. John R. Dunning, former professor of physics at Columbia University and now dean of Columbia's School of Engineering, has to say about atomic development. Dr. Dunning, the first American to split the uranium-235 atom, observed:

... Nuclear energy should provide a new source of energy which can be added to the others and, as a scientist and an engineer, I believe that through this broad use of energy we have both a gradually expanding basis and an absolutely necessary foundation on which to build, if we are to ... make possible the good life for all peoples. ...

Unfortunately, every advance in knowledge is a two-edged sword which can be used either for good or evil. Atomic energy is no different in principle from any other developments. . . . The social responsibility for the way this knowledge is used is only in small part that of the scientists. It is a responsibility which comes squarely back to everyone. The businessmen, the diplomats, the politicians, the lawyers, the military groups, all must bear their share. The clergy especially have a serious role, and and the teachers at every level. . . .

The responsibility for the way the social order uses knowledge *belongs to everyone.*

Obviously, then, the future course of all mankind will be profoundly affected by this tremendous power. Many people tend to think of it only in terms of defense or destruction. But there is much more to it than that. We are dealing with a great discovery about *the fundamental nature of everything physical.*

WHAT "SPLITTING THE ATOM" MEANS

When an atom is "split," the heart of the atom—the nucleus—undergoes a change. In this process of changing, atom radiation results. Tremendous heat is released. Not heat at temperatures in the thousands of degrees—as when coal, for instance, is burned—but heat in temperatures at *millions* of degrees. All over the country this process of splitting the atom is going forward day in and day out on a huge scale in America's atomic centers. Heat, however, does not change the various elements. Transmutation of the elements results from the addition or subtraction of nuclear particles.

To give some further idea of the tremendous potential of atomic energy, consider the radiation power of rays from, say, radium and X-ray machines. Everyone knows how powerful these rays are. Everyone knows, too, that radium is scarce and machines extremely costly. *But just the by-products of three or four weeks' operation in one of our atomic centers is the*

equivalent of tons of radium and gives off more radiation than
all the X-ray machines in the world combined.

TREMENDOUS POSSIBILITIES

So far, all the attention—or almost all—has been given the damage that this radiation can produce. The industrial and technical uses to which huge amounts of radiation can be put have not yet been fully explored. But this much is obvious. *The possibilities of the industrial atom would seem to be almost limitless.*

By the application of temperature, catalysts, and pressure, modern chemists have "rearranged" the atoms of such ordinary substances as chlorine, coal tar, and sulphur, thereby producing a series of more than *half a million new compounds.* Some of these compounds already have found their use in industry. As time goes on and our knowledge increases, atomic energy and its by-products can literally make over the world in which we live.

IN THE FIELD OF MEDICINE

In the field of medicine, as in agriculture, the surface of the enormous potential in atomic energy which can be utilized has scarcely been scratched. However, it is recognized that the detection and cure of various diseases and disabilities is a distinct possibility in the not-too-distant future. Even now such a crippling ailment as hardening of the arteries is yielding to detection long before the disease reaches its advanced stages—this through atomic research.

Not long ago a young ex-GI was stricken with an incurable disease. As the months went by he gradually grew weaker and weaker. There seemed to be absolutely no hope for him. And then one day a friend urged him to try one of the new treatments developed from experiments in the atomic field. The young man agreed and was taken to a Veterans Hospital. Within a few weeks he was able to return home. Now he is back on his job and leading a normal life.

THE POWER IN OUR HANDS

To those who think that the discovery and development of atomic energy was more or less accidental and that only the scientists and chemists and physicists should be concerned with it, the observations of one young scientist should provide additional food for thought.

"The more I work," he said, "the more I am convinced that inventions, discoveries, events—nothing happens by chance, but that each fits into God's plan for the universe. Down through the ages discoveries and inventions have been brought about just when we've needed them most.

"I believe atomic energy fits into God's concept. God has withheld such knowledge until He thought it suitable and usable at this stage of our civilization. Atomic energy, of course, has its destructive side, as has practically every other force ever revealed. Medicine, for example, can be used to kill or to cure, depending into whose hands it falls. Atomic energy, under the direction of man's free will, can also relieve suffering and misery, can revolutionize industry, can make fertile barren lands.

"I am sure that God did not reveal atomic energy to destroy man but to help him, to heal him, to provide for his temporal needs. . . ."

OPPORTUNITIES—NOW AND IN THE FUTURE

At the present time there are, of course, only a limited number of openings in the atomic-energy field. However, it can be reasonably expected that eventually there may be places for hundreds of thousands. No one can foretell the number of opportunities which the splitting of the atom will unfold as the various phases of atomic development go forward.

This much is certain, however. In addition to scientific and technical workers, atomic energy will demand men and women to staff the numerous offices—clerks, typists, stenographers, et cetera—as well as those in the semiskilled and unskilled classifications. By his very presence, even the least worker in the field can be an instrument of grace and bring God's blessing down on it.

Atomic energy can be—will be—what we make of it. It should be used for the advancement of our civilization and the benefit of all mankind. To bring this about, men and women of high purpose and dedication to the ideals upon which America was founded are needed to take up lifetime careers in this vital field.

2.

Your Part in This Vital Field

The atomic-energy program calls for bold moves, for rapid progress. This is especially important in the field of basic nuclear science. It is no secret that our great structure of nuclear technology has been built on an extraordinarily slim foundation of basic knowledge about the atom nucleus.

We have already mentioned what reaction takes place when an atom is "split"—the heat that is released, et cetera. And while the splitting of the atom is an accomplished fact, the battle, so to speak, has only just begun. Without our going into a technical discussion on the subject—which is not our purpose here, nor a matter on which we are qualified to write —nevertheless we may be able to give you some idea of the formidability of the job when we point out that an atom is so small that *one hundred billion, billion of them are contained in the head of a pin!*

Not only that, but the nucleus—the object of study in nuclear science—is about *ten thousand times smaller than the atom.* If an atom were expanded to the size of a concert hall, its central nucleus would be smaller than a housefly. The nucleus constitutes nearly all the mass of the atom and, consequently, *the mass of all things.* A piece of solid nuclear material the size of a child's marble would weigh more than two hundred million tons!

AN ANSWER TO THE SKEPTICS

Because the world of science has made this tremendous discovery, there are some people who feel that we are knocking at the final doors of the ultimate mystery of Creation and that when those doors are opened all things will be known to them. In their blindness they have come to believe that God has somehow become unnecessary.

To such people the words of Thomas E. Murray, a member of the Atomic Energy Commission, delivered at the commencement exercises at Marquette University, June 11, 1950, should make effective answer. Mr. Murray observed:

> With each new discovery our sense of mystery and our need for God grow more profound; and our wonder is abandoned to wider areas in which we can get lost. How can the idea of an omnipotent God seem foreign or fabulous to a civilization which holds a kind of ingrown infinity in the head of a pin; or who beholds in the Milky Way a mere outpost of far-flung space? . . .
>
> If fusion and fission are misdirected to the service of destruction and waste, that is man's fault, not God's. Man simply discovers and invents. By definition the inventor is one who finds. So is the discoverer. Something has to be hidden before it can be found. Something has to be there before it can be discovered. It is God Who has hidden and it is God Who has put something there. It has taken centuries for man to discover God's Atom. . . .

RAPID EXPANSION

In all, about eight million dollars is likely to be spent for physical research this year through "off-site" contracts—that is, in contracts to various universities and a few concerns scattered around the country. An additional twenty-three million dollars will be spent in the various major atomic-energy research laboratories—this for salaries and laboratory-operating expenses, plus, occasionally, the cost of some minor equipment. Another twenty-five million dollars is currently being spent on the construction of new physical-research facilities and equipment.

SURPRISING BUT TRUE

For those whose thoughts on atomic energy are confined to the memory of the terrible destruction visited on Hiroshima and Nagasaki, the statement by President Truman that more lives have been saved by the development of atomic energy than have been destroyed may come as somewhat of a surprise.

No less an authority than the Atomic Energy Commission has stated that through the use of *radioisotopes* alone doctors are discovering things they never knew before about how the human body works and how diseases develop.

Thyroid glands are being studied by means of *radioiodine*.

Heart failures, studied with *radiosodium,* have been shown to be complicated in some cases by an accumulation of sodium. New treatment for some types of heart trouble already has brought relief to many.

Cancer is being studied intensively in new ways with the use of *radiocarbon*.

New drugs—the sulfa group, penicillin, et cetera—are being set aside for further study also.

As more hospitals and laboratories obtain the equipment and personnel they need to initiate and continue research, the flood of information is bound to grow. That information means a longer and healthier life for millions of men, women, and children all over the earth.

TECHNICIANS NEEDED

With the field opening up on such a wide front, the need for technologists to work in the production end of atomic development has not yet been met. Those who may be "sparked" to take up careers in atomic energy as trained personnel with a Christopher purpose should find the following listing of job classifications helpful:

1. *The Industrial Physician*—assigned to atomic-energy plants—must have knowledge of radioactivity.

2. *The Industrial Nurse*—must be specially trained for the job.

3. *The Radiologist*—trained in the detection, measurement, evaluation, and analysis of radioactive materials.

4. *The Pharmacist*—trained to handle new drugs.

5. *The Veterinarian*—who must have knowledge of radioactivity in order to handle animals for experimental purposes.

6. *The Health Physicist*—a new type of specialist resulting from atomic-energy development.

7. *Laboratory Assistants*—who receive on-the-job training to assist those in any of the above categories.

8. *Medico-Physicist*—to conduct research in changes in human bodies occurring as a result of exposure to radiation.

9. *Nuclear Engineer*—competent to work in development of atomic power.

10. *Chemical Process Engineer*—trained to separate radioactive materials.

ALLIED FIELDS

The allied industries of *pharmaceutical research* and *drug manufacturing* will likewise have need of additional personnel to keep pace with new developments and techniques in the area of administration and testing of medicinal products. The specific research fields in this division are those of *biology, biochemistry, physiology,* and *therapy.*

In the division of *Natural Science* more personnel will be required in the fields of *bacteriology, plant physiology,* and *animal physiology and pathology.*

Engineering, one of the most vital divisions of the field, will likewise have new branches opened up, due to atomic advancement, as time goes by. It will make new demands on scientists, mechanics, toolmakers, administrative and clerical help. Civil

engineers, chemical engineers, metallurgists, mechanical, auto-
motive, mining, and electrical engineers, radio and archi-
tectural specialists, to give but a partial listing, will all be
needed in increasing numbers. In fact, many positions are open
at the present time for those who are suitably qualified.

INDUSTRIAL POSSIBILITIES

The most obvious peacetime use of atomic energy is as a
producer of *power*. One pound of uranium or plutonium can
yield about 2,600,000 kilowatt-hours of energy.

Atomic energy could have many advantages if and when it
becomes cheap and widespread. The black pall of smoke over
many of our cities might be lifted, and a general improvement
in health could result. Atomic energy could greatly influence
the use of power not only in our country but could provide
power for undeveloped countries abroad and consequently
raise their standard of living.

Even in *transportation* there is a definite possibility that
atomic energy may sometime be used. At the moment there are
many obstacles to using such energy in, say, automobiles. But
supersized aircraft may be fitted out with power plants, and
atomic-powered trains may be possible, though not likely to
be tried out for some time.

AGRICULTURAL DEVELOPMENT

One of the great mysteries in the scientific world is how
plants perform what is known as *photosynthesis*. Photosynthesis is the transformation of carbon dioxide and water into
sugar and then into starch. The ability of plants to do this,
using sunlight as the energy source, is the basis for the food
supply of every living thing on the earth.

By using radioactive carbon-dioxide gas to surround plants,
biologists can trace what happens to the carbon as it is "built"
into the plants.

The riddle, of course, is by no means solved, but we are on
the way. And once we discover the *why* and *how* of photo-

synthesis, the problem of synthesizing food and fuel directly from cheap and abundant chemical products will be determined.

BENEFITS TO LIVESTOCK

In regard to the effects of atomic energy on livestock—through agricultural development—already new information is being gained that will mean lower cost for livestock growers. For example, radioactive cobalt is being used to study one form of anemia in animals. The lack of small amounts of cobalt in the soil has been responsible for this condition in grazing livestock. Scientists have known this for years, but now radiocobalt has shown that cobalt applied with fertilizer does not stay with the animal long. Therefore, sheep and cattle that are deficient in cobalt must be supplied with the element constantly.

Radiocopper has shown that cattle are unable to make use of the phosphorus they need if they are deficient in copper.

Radiophosphorus is being used to study range paralysis in fowl.

NEW PLANT GROWTH

In the broad area of plant life, there is the possibility of producing new species of plants by bombarding plant seeds with various kinds of rays. Some of the mutations, or permanent changes in species, produced thereby might prove extremely valuable. Furthermore, radioactivity would not only make it possible to speed up nature's rate of desirable mutations but might also give us a better understanding of the whole mechanism and development of organisms.

WORKERS NEEDED

All the foregoing has been set forth so that some idea of the magnitude and complexity of the atomic-energy field and its power for good may be realized.

Certain specialized job categories have been listed to acquaint those with high purpose with the opportunities in the field. In the next section a more comprehensive listing of the entire employment picture will be given, with emphasis on the *non-technical* as well as on the technical positions to be sought.

All jobs are important in this vital sphere—administrative, clerical, and non-skilled as well as highly specialized occupations.

As with the other fields of influence—government, education, labor, communications, and social service—atomic energy will be exactly what we make of it. If enough men and women with a Christlike purpose go in and dedicate themselves to lifetime careers in the field, there to work for the betterment of all mankind, the extent of their changing the world for the better can truly know no bounds.

Far from being a force to be viewed with fear and misgiving, atomic energy is just one more demonstration of the love that the Creator of all has for each and every one of His creatures. It is our responsibility to use this gift properly. If we don't, we may not survive to get a second chance.

3.

Job Opportunities

Jobs in the atomic-energy field are not basically different from other opportunities in government service. However, there are two points of difference: (1) If a person is in the technical branch of atomic energy, he must have specialized training not found in some other occupations; and (2) *all* the jobs in atomic-energy work are more important than comparable jobs in almost any other line of endeavor.

The first point of difference needs no explanation. The second point, since it is so all-inclusive, may require some additional comment.

To give you an idea why all job classifications in this vital field are so important, consider the precautions which are taken, for example, at Atomic Energy Headquarters in Washington to insure the utmost security in its operations. These precautions apply to working personnel and visitors alike.

Situated on Constitution Avenue, the building is one of the best-guarded structures in the world. Specially trained and selected guards, armed, and schooled in judo tactics, are stationed inside and outside the building. Special electric alarm systems protect every window. Electric "eyes" are posted all over the outside of the building and atop it. Anything heavier than hailstones, birds, or leaves will set off an alarm.

Tamperproof badges and passes are used by all personnel from the top officials down to the newest office boy. These badges, containing the wearer's photograph encased in a special plastic case, are not allowed to leave the building. An employee, upon entering the building, presents a plastic, non-counterfeitable card at a window and receives in exchange another plastic photo badge to be attached to the lapel. The face of the employee can then be scrutinized and compared with his likeness on the badge.

On leaving the building, each employee must turn in his badge at the door, and it is reissued to the wearer only in exchange for the plastic, non-counterfeitable card mentioned above. Thus there is no opportunity for anyone to lose his badge outside the building, where someone might find it and substitute another photograph.

STRINGENT STANDARDS

All told, there are thousands of special guards currently assigned to the physical protection of Atomic Energy Headquarters and its field installations. Stringent standards have resulted in an unusually high type of personnel for this work. At the Los Alamos Atomic Center, for example, out of fourteen thousand applicants for guard duty only *one thousand* were able to qualify.

Not only are security officers on duty wherever Atomic Energy Commission plants are operating, but the Federal Bureau of Investigation maintains resident agents on the sites to handle the responsibilities for which it is charged under the Atomic Energy Act. The contractors who actually operate the production facilities incidental to atomic development (such as General Electric, Westinghouse, et cetera) have additional details of guards and security safeguards.

INTEGRITY OF THE INDIVIDUAL

To an extraordinarily high degree, then, atomic-energy development and research depends on the integrity of the individual, from the most obscure clerk to the head of the Atomic Energy Commission itself. The newspaper headlines of recent months, with respect to violations of security by men like the English scientist, Dr. Klaus Fuchs, in the top ranks of atomic research, down to a courier like Harry Gold, are examples of what we mean. A clerk, or any person who has charge of or access to confidential papers, could extract whatever information he wished from such documents and use it for his own purposes. By the time the loss was discovered, irreparable damage could be done.

From top to bottom, atomic energy should be staffed only by the most competent, conscientious, sound-thinking men and women. Each and every one should be dominated by a deep sense of loyalty and service to God and country.

THOSE ALREADY IN THE FIELD

As of April 1950 there were 61,088 persons employed in the atomic-energy program in the United States. This total is broken down as follows:

Direct Atomic Energy Commission Employees	4,894
(763 of which are in Washington, D.C.)	
Contractor Employees	56,194
Total	61,088

This total is further broken down into the following occupational classifications:

Scientific and Technical	7,330	or	12%
Management and Supervisory	4,276	or	7%
Administrative	12,217	or	20%
Skilled	15,885	or	26%
Semiskilled	10,995	or	18%
Unskilled	10,385	or	17%
Total	61,088		100%

As was mentioned earlier, job opportunities in the field are limited at the moment. But there is ample reason to believe that further scientific development will lead to an inestimably larger number of openings in fields outside the immediate operations of the Atomic Energy Commission itself. These openings will by no means be confined to those with technical or scientific training. They will include all categories of work.

Obviously, then, the field is vast and, in fact, expanding so rapidly that we can touch only in general on the various types of job classification. To acquaint the prospective careerist in the atomic-energy field with these possibilities, we submit the following brief explanation of what each job division covers: [1]

SCIENTIFIC AND TECHNICAL

All scientific and engineering personnel. This includes physicians, dentists, architects, and designers.

MANAGEMENT AND SUPERVISORY

All the higher levels of management and supervision, such as managers, superintendents, division, department, and branch heads.

[1] In addition to the following job analysis, the Atomic Energy Commission has established a system of scholarships and fellowships in physical, biological, and medical sciences in order to increase the number of *trained* personnel in the various fields *in* and *associated with* atomic energy.

ADMINISTRATIVE

Office workers, including clerical employees, accountants, auditors, stenographers, timekeepers, buyers, draftsmen, and professions not otherwise included, such as lawyers, teachers, et cetera.

SKILLED

Mechanics and craftsmen at both the journeyman and foreman level, who have had a specific long-term training for their work, such as machinists, toolmakers, glass blowers, electricians, pipe fitters, insulators, bricklayers, and instrument makers.

SEMISKILLED

Mechanics and operators with limited skill and qualified through a comparatively brief period of training, such as chemical and research operators, minor laboratory technicians, craft apprentices, air-tool operators, instrument checkers, et cetera.

UNSKILLED

Laborers, janitors, watchmen, trades helpers, warehousemen, laundry and cafeteria workers, and others for whom practically no special training is required.

NOT CIVIL SERVICE

Employment in the atomic-energy field under the direction of the Atomic Energy Commission does *not* come under the Civil Service classification. This fact is mentioned in order to avoid needless confusion for persons who wish to take up lifetime career work in the field but who are uncertain where to apply.

If a person wishes to work for the AEC in Washington, D.C., obviously his application for employment should be made direct to that headquarters. If employment is desired in one of the laboratories or research centers doing atomic-energy work, application should be made to the laboratory or research center concerned. If employment is sought in one of the contractors' plants which operate production facilities for atomic energy, application should likewise be made to the plant directly.

The Atomic Energy Commission maintains three national laboratories: *Argonne National Laboratory,* operated by the University of Chicago in DuPage County, Illinois; *Oak Ridge National Laboratory,* operated by Carbide and Carbon Chemicals Corporation, at Oak Ridge, Tennessee; and *Brookhaven National Laboratory,* operated by Associated Universities, Incorporated, at Upton, Long Island, New York. In addition it has many other research centers, including the following:

Knolls Atomic Power Laboratory, operated by General Electric Company, at Schenectady and West Milton, New York.

Los Alamos Scientific Laboratory, operated by University of California at Los Alamos, New Mexico.

Mound Laboratory, operated by Monsanto Chemical Company at Miamisburg, Ohio.

Sandia Laboratory, operated by the Sandia Corporation at Albuquerque, New Mexico.

Westinghouse Atomic Power Division Laboratories, operated by Westinghouse Electric Corporation at Bettis Field, near Pittsburgh, Pennsylvania.

OTHER INSTALLATIONS

Four other installations are maintained on university campuses, with buildings and equipment financed in large part by the commission and with staff and supply expenses wholly reimbursed. These installations are: (1) Ames Laboratory, Iowa State College, Ames, Iowa; (2) Radiation Laboratory (including Donner Laboratory of Medical Physics and Crocker Laboratory) operated by University of California at Berkeley, California; (3) Rochester Atomic Energy Project (biological and medical research only) operated by the University of Rochester, Rochester, New York; (4) UCLA Atomic Energy

Project (biological and medical research only) operated by University of California at Los Angeles, California.

ONLY PART OF THE PICTURE

Such installations as the above, financed in the main by the government, constitute only a part of the picture. Exclusive of reactor development, about 15 per cent, or four million dollars, of the commission's physical-research budget during the fiscal year 1949 was for work carried on by scholars on the staffs and in the laboratories of many universities, research institutes, industrial organizations, and government agencies other than the commission.

VAST PROGRAM

All in all, the program of the Atomic Energy Commission is so vast that it is impossible to do more than touch on the "high spots" in the short space at our command. But it should be mentioned again, even at the risk of being repetitious, that *all types of jobs* in this vital field—though not necessarily with the AEC proper—are open in limited number now, and there is every reason to hope that there will be many, many more openings in the future.

These jobs will not be for scientists, researchers, chemists, medical men, and technicians alone. Clerks, typists, office workers, guards—all these will be needed, and all are tremendously important. The smallest piece of vital information misused or placed in the wrong hands can do far-reaching harm. By the same token, such information used properly can work for the benefit of all mankind.

4.

Instructing Our Young

Some months ago a high-school student in New York who had asked the Atomic Energy Commission in Washington for certain information on its activities and program sent the following letter of thanks for its prompt reply:

DEAR SIRS:

Thanks for the speeches and literature you sent. This coming Thursday we are having a Natural Science Club Meeting at school and I am going to use one of those speeches you sent me. I think you will agree that it will be a good way to start the Meeting off with a "bang." You know, it really is a very funny thing, but every time something is mentioned about atomic energy at our Meetings, everyone seems to turn green around the gills. I guess it is because none of them know much about the matter. That is why I am going to address the Club on atomic energy. . . .

This letter is reprinted to illustrate the necessity of educating the people of America, young folk in particular, to the part they are expected to play in the tremendously important field of atomic-energy development.

CONFIRMING TESTIMONY

Sumner T. Pike, a member of the U. S. Atomic Energy Commission, made this point emphatically clear. Speaking to a gathering of secondary-school principals on February 26, 1949, he said:

. . . Why do we consider . . . understanding of the whole subject of atomic energy so important—why is it that principals and teachers, particularly, should be well informed? [Because] in a very real sense you are training tomorrow's citizenship. Your students of today will be the voters of the next generation. Atomic energy is already bringing with it great questions of public policy. It will bring more. The proper handling of these problems will demand an informed public . . . so that we will not come to consider atomic energy the prerogative of the experts, and thus leave to others decisions which are properly the citizen's.

Children can understand atomic energy. It is not too deep nor too remote from their daily lives. As has been said so many times, once the people have the facts they can be depended upon to make wise and common-sense decisions. . . .

INSTRUCTING THE YOUNG

Repeatedly in our Christopher literature we have urged men and women of high purpose to go into the teaching profession, there to use—in a legitimate way—their influence for good.

To those already in the educational field or contemplating entering it, we would like to make this further recommendation in the light of what has been written above. *We urge them to become informed on atomic energy*, regardless of the subject matter with which they deal, so that they may become influences toward right thinking on this most important discovery of our age.

The students in our classrooms will need to know how the Atomic Energy Commission is carrying out its program as authorized by the Atomic Energy Act of 1946. They will want to know something of the magnitude of its operations, which extend from the Belgian Congo to Eniwetok atoll in the Pacific. They will want to know the reason for such extensive territorial operations. They will want to understand—and must understand—the program for safeguarding the national defense and security. They must be trained to comprehend, as lay people, the development of atomic power and the accumulation of new knowledge relating to this power, particularly in the fields of medicine, industry, and agriculture.

TECHNICAL UNDERSTANDING

In addition to the above, students will have to be informed on the simple physical facts of the atom and the processes whereby energy is released and controlled for man's benefit.

Generations of students have assimilated technical information in the fields of chemistry and physics without undue difficulty. They can do the same with atomic energy. They need not be nuclear physicists any more than they have to be experts in sound to understand the basic principles of radio.

Atomic energy is a tremendous new force that God has placed in our hands for the positive benefit of all mankind, as well as for our defense. This point cannot be stressed too often. As one atomic-energy authority stated not long ago: *"In spite of some of the wild predictions of the future which have been made, I think we are more apt to underestimate the effects of the atomic age upon our lives than to overestimate them."*

A START HAS BEEN MADE

An encouraging sign that a start has already been made to acquaint the youth of America with this new force is evident from the steps being taken toward this goal in various parts of the country.

In New York City there has been established the first atomic-energy teacher-training course in the United States sponsored by the Board of Education of the city in co-operation with the U. S. Atomic Energy Commission. In encouraging any and all teachers of the New York City system to attend, Dr. William Jansen, Superintendent of Schools, stated: "I want to emphasize that the course is intended for every member of our staff. We are all involved in the problems of this atomic age no matter what subjects we may teach. I do not know of any other subject that can be considered more important to the children of today than atomic energy."

The course in New York was attended by twelve hundred science and social-studies teachers. It considered the basic principles of atomic energy, its present benefits, its social and economic implications.

ALL OVER THE COUNTRY

New York is not alone in the effort to keep her teaching body informed on this important subject. In Nebraska, Iowa,

Kansas, Illinois, Pennsylvania, Michigan, Massachusetts, Rhode Island, and Virginia, to give a partial listing, serious and detailed study is going forward. All in all, it is a heartening sign of the educators' awareness of the need for intelligent and sound thinking about atomic energy.

WIDE SCOPE

It must be remembered, however, that all levels of education —not merely the science and social-studies departments—are affected by the discovery and development of atomic energy. History, geography, and even English will feel the repercussions. Engineering, mechanical-drawing, and shop classes will find their places in the field, and within the trades new opportunities are constantly arising as new skills are needed. The graphic arts, in the making of posters, exhibits, et cetera, have their specific contribution to make in the general education of the public.

Composition classes can utilize the broad field as well as the specific field influenced by atomic energy for their theme material. Librarians will need to keep pace with the growing body of material and must have a background in atomic energy in order to evaluate the material printed on the subject with a view to its scientific worth and its presentation from a standpoint of ethics.

THE NEED IS GREAT

Since, in dealing with atomic energy, we are face to face with the *fundamental nature of everything physical,* how this great force is used will depend on the number of spiritually minded, well-trained, patriotic men and women who make the field their personal concern.

Teachers in the classrooms can start to direct our youth toward these fields. Those who have left school and completed their formal education can yet be encouraged to think of transferring their abilities to the atomic-energy field. This applies both to technical and non-technical labor, for there will be countless opportunities for men and women of all types of

skills—clerks, typists, stenographers, accountants, et cetera—
to make atomic energy their full-time careers, these in addition to the scientists, chemists, physicists, medical men, researchers, and so on.

All jobs are important. Each and every one counts. Our world can either be destroyed or led to an unbelievably high level of progress and development by the manner in which atomic energy is used.

The future is in our hands. What we do with it will—*not* might—determine the course of history for the next thousand years.

FOR ADDITIONAL READING

An Act for the Development and Control of Atomic Energy (Atomic Energy Act of 1946) Public Law 585, 79th Congress. Washington, D.C.: Government Printing Office, 1946. 22 pp. $.05.

Isotopes . . . A Three-Year Summary of U. S. Distribution. Washington, D.C.: Government Printing Office, 1949. 201 pp. $.45.
    A report on the growth of isotopes distribution, their uses, and a bibliography of 1,850 papers on the utilization of pile-produced isotopes in medicine, animal physiology, bacteriology, animal husbandry, plant physiology, physics, chemistry, and industrial research.

EIDINOFF, DR. MAXWELL LEIGH, and RUCHLIS, HYMAN. *Atomics for the Millions.* Introduction by Harold C. Urey. New York: McGraw-Hill, 1947. 281 pp. $3.50.
    Traces the development of atomics from early Greek theory to a preview of the coming applications. For the layman who has no background of either physics or mathematics.

HECHT, SELIG. *Explaining the Atom.* New York: Viking, 1947. 205 pp. $3.00.

First, Second, Third, Fourth and Fifth Semiannual Reports of the U. S. Atomic Energy Commission to the Congress of the United States. Senate Documents Nos. 8, 96, 118,

199. 80th Congress and 81st Congress, respectively. Washington, D.C.: Government Printing Office, 1947–48.

POTTER, ROBERT D. *Young People's Book of Atomic Energy.* New York: Dodd, Mead, 1948. Revised edition. 181 pp. $2.50.

Account of Bikini tests; peaceful uses, economic and medical especially; and plans for international control. Major emphasis is on the physics of atomic energy and the development of the atomic bombs.

ROTHMANN, S. C., edited by. *Constructive Uses of Atomic Energy.* New York: Harper, 1949. 258 pp. $3.00.

A collection of fourteen articles by as many authors dealing with the possible uses of atomic energy in non-military fields. A technical book designed to dispel the common misconception that atomic energy is beyond the comprehension of the layman. Includes a bibliography and glossary of scientific terms.

STRENGTHENING COLLEGE TEACHING

1.

A Challenging Opportunity

One of the chief objectives of the Christopher movement from the very beginning has been to encourage the best type of Americans to take up careers in every branch of education, from kindergarten to university. As important as all these branches are, however, we feel that those on the *college and university* level deserve special attention because of their impact, for better or worse, on the lives of millions of our citizens.

At present there are 1,729 institutions of higher learning in the United States, whose total enrollment numbers slightly over 2,500,000 students. Each year these colleges and universities send some five hundred thousand young men and women into the main stream of American life.

Most people would agree, if they thought about it, that this training period is perhaps the most vital in the life of the average young person and therefore should be in the hands of those who are distinguished not only for competence but also for character, those who have a love and respect for the basic spiritual principles upon which our country depends for its continuance as a free nation.

Unfortunately, however, most of the American public have not given the matter much thought. Their attitude toward college teaching has been: "Let someone else take care of that." Not only have they taken the apathetic "Let George do it" stand, but in most instances they have not taken the trouble to find out who "George" is and whether he is teaching ideas that are good or bad. This habit, common to most free peoples today, of staying in the grandstand as a spectator instead of participating in the game of life has contributed greatly to the disaster which has devastated much of the earth these past few decades. The pagan, materialistic teachings of many colleges and universities, which have helped bring us to the edge of national catastrophe, have been themselves a result of the failure on our part to stress God-given fundamentals.

One example of the pagan, materialistic teachings to which we refer came our way through a letter from a woman who was studying at a teachers' college in the East. Knowing that we were concerned with the state of affairs in American educational life, she forwarded us this excerpt from a book, *Social Institutions,* by Lloyd Vernor Ballard of Beloit University (page 472):

> Supernaturalism in religion should be replaced by a naturalism in which man is recognized as a part of nature. Biblical cosmology has been destroyed by modern science. Biblical criticism has cut away the grounds for many ancient beliefs. Doctrines with respect to atonement, inspiration, incarnation, salvation, and judgment are no longer socially significant. The theological and metaphysical aspects of religion are important only to a few; for most men justice, fair dealing, an adequate income, and opportunities for self-development are vastly more important. Humanism rather than transcendentalism is required of organized religion. Religious beliefs should be frankly recognized as working hypotheses, the validity of which is found in works—results. Doctrinal authoritarianism in religion should be boldly labeled as wishful thinking, as defense mechanism, or as a power-technique.

DOING SOMETHING ABOUT IT

Rather than merely deplore this dangerous tendency, however, we decided to try to do something about it. We felt that large numbers of young persons would gladly devote their lives to teaching if there was ever brought home to them the tremendous service they could render in such a career. Often just a bit of emphasis on purpose and direction would suffice, we believed, to launch many a young person of high ideals into the rewarding career of a college instructor or professor.

One of our first attempts in this direction took place a few years ago in San Francisco. We met a young man there who was to complete his college course within two months. To our question as to what he intended to do after graduation, his reply was interesting, although painfully typical of millions of American youth. "Gosh, I don't know. Try and get a job and really make some money, I suppose. After all, isn't that what I'm being trained for?"

This defensive attitude was most revealing, since it indicated that, subconsciously, he believed he should have a purpose in life higher than mere money-making. Feeling that there was a great untapped capacity for good in him, we observed:

"It's easy to see you have a lot of fine ideas. Too bad you aren't aiming for a job where you can put them to work for the benefit of all, instead of suppressing them. A few more years of training and you could become an instructor at California or Stanford or some other university. Then over the years you could pass along your sound ideas to thousands of young people. There wouldn't be much glamour in it, I know, and it's certain you won't make your fortune, but you would do far more than merely earn a living. You'd have the satisfaction, for time and for eternity, of knowing the world has been made a bit better because you've been in it."

The student didn't answer for a moment or two. Then slowly his face lighted up and a grin broke the corners of his mouth. "I think you've got something there," he said. "It sounds like a good idea. But that's the first time I ever thought of it that way."

A short while after this incident I happened to be in Los Angeles at a meeting of fifteen young college graduates. During the course of my brief talk I pleaded with them to develop a true appreciation for the important role the teacher must play in American life if our country is to remain free. After I finished, one young man came up to me and said quietly: "This changes my whole outlook. I never before thought of teaching in this way. If it hadn't been for what you said, I'd probably have muffed an opening as an instructor at Cal. Tech. that was offered me recently. My parents, my friends, practically everybody I knew told me I'd be crazy to take up a life of teaching. You're the first one who has told me otherwise. I'm taking the job!"

THERE IS A CONNECTION

If more people could understand that there is an intimate connection between the wrong kind of education and the recurring wars which plague mankind, a start in the right direction would not be long in coming. Every few decades millions of young Americans offer their lives, willing to *die* for peace. A much smaller number, willing to *live* for peace, here and over the world, could achieve more in the teaching field than most realize.

There is little danger of exaggerating the power for good that rests in the hands of a teacher. Students put implicit faith in him. Whatever is in his head—good or bad—passes into theirs. Nearly all drink in as gospel truth every pronouncement the teacher makes, seldom knowing whether what he gives them is the truth or not. They accept him as the final authority.

OUR RESPONSIBILITY

To see that this authority is not abused or confused, there rests on the rank and file of good Americans a serious responsibility. If the teachers in our colleges—and in all departments of education, for that matter—do not come from our midst, then we are handing over the future of our country to those who, through stupidity, lack of proper values, or determined treachery, would undermine our nation. Such a conclusion is inescapable, for it is these types of people who are going into the teaching profession in ever-increasing numbers.

If, however, we can work fast enough to supplement the ranks of those able, high-principled teachers in the profession who are still faithful to their duties, the present dangerous trend can yet be changed for a better, more hopeful one.

THREE EXAMPLES

Among many examples showing what men and women with high purpose are doing in the field of education right now, the following few are typical of those who are dedicating themselves to the teaching profession in order to leave the world a bit better than they found it, who are daily carrying Christ into the dust and heat of the market place.

A REAL SACRIFICE

In Texas a young member of the faculty of the University of Houston has been "giving his all" in the teaching field. So much so, in fact, that he has passed up a standing offer of a job at twenty-five thousand dollars a year from a large automobile corporation in order to continue teaching (at a salary of six thousand dollars a year).

FROM LAWYER TO TEACHER

A fairly successful lawyer who had practiced some five years after being admitted to the bar caught enough of the Christopher idea to give up his practice and take a post in one of our midwestern universities, teaching law. His purpose was not just to instruct young attorneys in the intricacies of legal procedure, however. As far as possible, he has made it his business to encourage them to take up careers in labor law rather than in the more financially rewarding practice of corporation law, since he sees in the first field a greater opportunity to bring Christopher principles to bear. Not long ago a student whom he'd taught, but whom he hadn't seen in a number of years, came to see him. He'd taken this lawyer's advice and was reporting back now to thank him. *"I've never regretted my decision,"* he offered. *"Others in my class probably have made more money, but I'm certain not one of them has experienced the sense of satisfaction that's come my way. I really get a kick out of what I'm doing . . . and I think God does too!"*

A Negro girl, a graduate of the University of California, accepted a position in a small college in the deep South despite all efforts of her friends to persuade her to the contrary. To their arguments that she would be most unhappy in her new surroundings, she replied: "I don't see how my people can be helped unless we who know Christ go to them, share their problems, teach them. We who have been more fortunate haven't any right to use what we have just for ourselves. I feel pretty strongly about that. We've got to get out and share. I can do that by teaching."

THE CHRISTOPHER THESIS

Every teacher who would bring Christ into the market place should take to heart the example of people like these. The teacher with a Christopher purpose should make every effort to *adapt* and *adopt* for his or her own use the very factors which underlie the success of the godless materialists, namely: *clear aims, hard work, a sense of dedication,* and *initiative.*

It is the Christopher thesis that, to be an effective force for good, each person must recognize clearly that he can be God's instrument in bringing His Truth even to the least of men. A reminder of how great a privilege this is can be found in the words of Daniel Webster, who, in an address given at Faneuil Hall in Boston in 1852, said:

If we work upon marble, it will perish.
If we work upon brass, time will efface it.

If we rear temples, they will crumple to dust.
But if we work upon men's immortal minds,
If we imbue them with high principles,
With the just fear of God and love of their fellow man,
We engrave on those tablets something which no time
can efface,
And which will brighten and brighten to all eternity.

2.

Who Will Teach Them?

When Alger Hiss was convicted of perjury, *Time* magazine made this interesting comment: "A brilliant but weak man had proved unworthy of the great trust placed in him. A fine talent had been put to doing evil. By the jury's verdict he was marked as a man who, having dedicated himself to Communism under a warped sense of idealism, had not served it openly, but covertly; a man who, having once served an alien master, lacked the courage to recant his past, but went on making of his whole life an intricate calculated lie."

When Klaus Fuchs, "an inoffensive-looking man of twisted brilliance," openly admitted that he had betrayed United States atomic secrets to Russia, a large number of Americans were frankly disturbed. Again, when Harry Gold, "a mild, shy man with a dilettante's interest in symphonic music and the ballet," who had graduated with honors from college, freely confessed that he had transmitted stolen atomic information to Fuchs, the rank and file of Americans winced once more. They had become so accustomed in recent years to associating extraordinary crimes with the ignorant and the illiterate that they had difficulty convincing themselves that those with the highest educational advantages could sink so low.

This lack of awareness on the part of most Americans is not

surprising. In recent years our country has been caught unprepared by attacks from *without*—first at Pearl Harbor, then in Korea. Yet a far more disastrous attack has been taking place on our society from *within*. This has been eating its way into the foundations of our nation for several decades—long before Communism appeared on the scene in any strength. This has stealthily gone about the task of undermining one support of Christian democracy after another.

IN THE FIELD OF EDUCATION

This has been a moral decay, a moral breakdown, which has reached into every segment of society and has made marked inroads into the field of *education*.

This attack hasn't happened by chance. It has been carefully promoted by a handful of atheists and agnostics who decided quite some time ago that they were going to reach the whole world with their godless ideas. They picked the college and university field here and abroad as the channel most suited to a wide dissemination of their theories. Their technique was to despiritualize the hundreds of thousands who would have the benefit of higher education, reasoning that once the great mass of people were cut off from spiritual concepts, they would be willing prey for any perverted or subverted ideology.

Some educators have seen only too well the purpose of the godless tactics and have spoken out to their countrymen in warning. Just recently Dr. George F. Zook, retiring after sixteen years as president of the American Council on Education, stated: *"One of the most distressing developments of the past century has been the growing tendency to separate education and religion."*

ATHEISM NOT THE ONLY PROBLEM

Not all of the blame for this tendency can be laid at the door of this handful of atheists, agnostics, or Communists. It is a dangerous oversimplification to think that the removal of such people from teaching positions will do away with the difficulties cropping up in our educational system. The problem is much deeper than that.

To begin with, we must recognize that secularism—which is life lived in practical forgetfulness of God—is a virus. It is by no means interested in attacking only those organisms which are run down. The virus of secularism seeks out not only the *easy* prey—those schools whose hold upon our Christian heritage has never been remarkably strong—it seeks also to enter and destroy the eminently *healthy* organisms—those schools (Catholic and non-Catholic alike) whose very lifeblood is religion. And to a surprising extent it succeeds.

The virus of secularism is insidious. It works by stealth. It continually varies its point and mode of attack. At the very moment that those who are responsible for the spiritual health of the college are resisting its thrusts at one point, this virus quietly creeps into another area where it can continue its deadly work of infecting the minds of faculty and student body.

It poisons many souls, distorting their sense of values, giving them an unhealthy concept of the meaning of success. It produces a delirium in which one's whole outlook on life turns topsy-turvy. First things—the spiritual—become last. Last things—material advantage, physical possessions—take first place. In its fevered confusion, the mind loses perspective. Religion becomes a Sunday affair with little or no relation to daily life.

This distortion affects even those whose resistance is unusually strong. These, though they retain their values, lose all desire to apply them to the life of our times. On others the effect of this virus takes even more subtle forms. As one commentator has put it, "They get so wrapped up in fighting communism and totalitarianism that they forget something far more important: the need for a decent, just Christian social order and the restoration of all things in Christ."

Occasionally this secularistic outlook makes a great deal of headway before those in charge of the college become aware of its presence. But sooner or later, thank God, someone is alerted to its encroachment. A teacher at one large university conducted under religious auspices said not long ago: "We woke up just in time. A few of us suddenly became aware that our school had gradually become a secularist institution with a religious veneer. The moment of that realization was the moment of our first real hope. You can't meet a challenge until you see what the challenge is."

It is easy to see, then, that atheism, agnosticism, Communism are only partial phases of the problem. Actually the situation is much more the result of creeping secularism than of any other cause.

This point was brought home to us by a brilliant professor at the University of California who had been teaching the Communist line in his classroom for nine years before he realized his mistake. He admitted that it took him a long time to realize that Communism did little more than increase discord and confusion by its destructive theories. Then he added that he knew hundreds of other young college teachers who were pretty much "in the same bucket" as himself before he came to his senses. He claimed that they, for the most part, were well intentioned but had little or no religious foundation because their college training had failed to provide it. Consequently they were "sitting ducks" for any strong idea that came along. They were groping for something to which to cling and, without realizing it, they were sucked in by the leftist surge. "They don't really mean any harm," he concluded, "but, as I used to do myself, they are teaching a lot of fuzzy ideas that are bound to mean trouble in the future."

ABUNDANT EVIDENCE

There is abundant evidence of this godless trend in American education for anyone wishing to examine it:

1. One professor, Harry Elmer Barnes, whose textbooks are used extensively throughout the United States, maintains the theory, as one observer put it, that *Christianity is the source of most of our social evils; that conversion to godlessness would make a better society; and that the ideas of soul, heaven,*

hell, immortality, sin, prayer, spiritual things, and the notions of the sacred are "cultural fossils in orthodoxy." This thesis is identical with the totalitarian philosophy, expressed by Hitler so bluntly: *"The Ten Commandments have lost their validity. . . . There is no such thing as Truth, either in the moral or in the scientific sense."*

2. At a well-known teacher's college not long ago, the questions asked in one examination paper used by graduate and undergraduate students alike followed the same line of perverted reasoning which Adolf Hitler employed to destroy all idea of sexual morality. Of course Hitler was most specific in explaining his purpose. As he wrote in *Mein Kampf:* *"Look at these young men and boys! What material! I shall eradicate the thousands of years of human domestication. Brutal youth —that is what I am after . . . I want to see once more in its eyes the gleam . . . of the beast of prey. With these I can make a new world . . . and create a new order."*

3. In *The Government of Modern States* a well-known professor observes: *"What we now speak of as individual liberties are merely the liberties which the state, as a matter of policy or expediency, determines shall be left to individual determination. . . . At any moment the state, acting through the machinery it has provided for itself, can enter this field and cancel the powers that it has granted or permitted . . ."* This book also asserts that the state is supreme; that it not only gives ultimate validity to all laws but determines the scope of its own legal powers and the way in which they will be exercised.

4. In one course at a university on the West Coast it is subtly denied that the human being has any free will, and it is asserted that he is, therefore, not to blame for anything he does. Any lingering restraints outside the penalty of "getting caught" are gradually made to disappear in the youthful minds. It is stated that there is little or no difference between right and wrong. The door is opened to murder, suicide, rape, perjury, dishonesty, and all manner of violation of the natural

law upon which normal, peaceful society depends for its very survival.

IT INEVITABLY HAPPENS

Every system of education that deliberately excludes God reduces man to the level of the beast and thereby opens the floodgates of misery and destruction for countless millions of innocent people. It helps little that those who foster these debasing educational theories recognize their mistakes when it is too late.

Nazism was the product of many so-called intellectuals who led the way in banishing any spiritual notion of man. Yet here, too, these intellectuals had scarcely any idea of the Frankenstein's monster they were creating. One of them, Osvald Spengler, who was living at the time of Hitler's rise to power and was himself a noted philosopher and historian, was horrified at the result of his own teaching even before he was repudiated by the Nazis.

Aware that a similar situation was shaping up in America, in 1940 Walter Lippmann uttered these significant words when he addressed the American Association for the Advancement of Science:

Modern education rejects and excludes from the curriculum of necessary studies the whole religious tradition of the West . . . thus there is an enormous vacuum where until a couple of decades ago there was the substance of education . . . there is no common faith, no common moral and intellectual discipline.

Newspaper columnist George Sokolsky lent weight to Lippmann's testimony not long ago when he told his readers:

. . . atheism may be taught our children, but not the word of God, not the Bible, not the Psalms, not the prophets, not the Apostles. Karl Marx is legal in schools but not Isaiah, or St. Mark. They suffer from biblical affiliation.

For many this is a serious question. They say that religion has no place in the schools. BUT HAS ANTI-RELIGION A PLACE?

Consider, finally, the observation of Dr. Ernest C. Colwell, president of the University of Chicago, which appeared in a recent news item in the New York *Times,* that the institutions of higher learning in this country *"throw their weight against religion by disclaiming involvement in religious matters."*

"The dominant attitude of the university faculty toward religion is one of indifference or carefully controlled neutrality," Dr. Colwell declared, *"with the result that the student concludes education is an area that does not need religion."*

Emphasizing that the college graduate carries this attitude into the business world and is *"easily persuaded that business does not need religion either,"* Dr. Colwell went on: *"As a result, religion is progressively banished from all the important areas of living."*

And he concluded: *"The urgent problem before us is how can the great American universities serve God more than they serve the devil? . . . Religion and morals must become the important and pervasive element in all education and inquiry."*

A HOPEFUL SOLUTION

How can this be accomplished? How can religion and morals become "the important and pervasive element in all education and inquiry," as Dr. Colwell testified they must?

The answer was given us by Christ Himself when He told us to "go" and keep "going" with His truth to mankind the world over.

The fact that we haven't followed His command to date should spur us on *now* to make up for our past negligence. A change for the better will come only when those with strong *spiritual* convictions make it their business to show an even greater devotion and zeal as daring apostles for their cause than is exhibited by those who, denying God, would wreck our civilization. As the proportion of men and women fired with a love of God and country increases among the 125,486 teachers now on the staffs of American colleges, universities, and teachers' training schools, to that extent will college education become more spiritual. Then one day in the not-too-distant future they may help our institutions of higher learning become what Newman, in *The Idea of a University*, said they should be: "... *a place where inquiry is pushed forward and discoveries verified and perfected, and rashness rendered innocuous and error exposed by the collision of mind with mind and knowledge with knowledge.*"

They may make as the watchword of our colleges the motto which Harvard University was given at its founding, one hundred and forty years before the signing of the Declaration of Independence: *In Christi Gloriam* (For the Glory of Christ). Incidentally, at that stage in our country's history, and during the administration of the school's first president, Master Dunster, one of the student directives was so explicit in emphasizing the spiritual values that characterized all phases of early American life that it bears repeating now. "*Let every student be plainly instructed,*" the directive read, "*and earnestly pressed to consider well, the maine end of his life and studies is to know God and Jesus Christ which is eternal life ... Christ [is] the only foundation of all sound knowledge and learning.*"

THE RESPONSIBILITY

Man's ascent through the ages has been long and hard, and at each step he has accumulated new knowledge about things, about people, about the relationship of men, one to another, in accordance with the Divine Plan.

Man is more than the collection of chemicals that atheists and agnostics say he is. Man is composed of body and soul, made to the image and likeness of God. To the whole human race can be applied with particular stress the words of Pope Pius XI in his *Encyclical on Christian Education*:

It must never be forgotten that the subject of Christian education is man whole and entire, soul united to body

*in unity of nature, with all his faculties, natural and
supernatural, such as right reason and revelation show
him to be. . . .*

Expressed another way, men are not born with clearly
formed ideas. The Christian philosophy of life does not flow
into man's soul without any outside stimulus. Man has a conscience, but it must be educated. And what better way is there
than through the medium of the teacher with high ideals, in
the classroom, on the campus, or in any one of a number of
different activities connected with school life?

3.

Motives and Qualities of the Christopher-minded College Teacher

Houston Peterson, in his book, *The Great Teachers* (page
341), Rutgers University Press, tells this story:

> While a lecture was going on before a large class, a
> student in the back row fell unquietly asleep. The pro-
> fessor noticed the defection but continued with his re-
> marks, more in sorrow than in anger. A few minutes
> later the boy recovered his consciousness and blurted out
> an apology. "No," said the professor, "it is I who should
> apologize to you—for not keeping you awake."

We retell this story to emphasize the qualities which a good
teacher should possess, especially a teacher who would work
in the vital educational field with a Christopher purpose. These
qualities were set forth quite clearly in an article entitled,
"Characteristics of the Good College Teacher," by Urban
Fleege, Ph.D. A good college teacher, the author points out:

1. *Is intellectually competent—master of his subject field, keeps abreast of developments, and has the capacity for analysis and synthesis.* This last is vital if he is to develop intellectual maturity in his students. Must have the "know-how" of approaching problems, breaking down ideas, relating them to neighboring concepts and building them up with his students into larger and more comprehensive patterns of knowledge.

2. *Fires the minds of his students with ideas, with aspirations, with visions of the Yet Unknown, with the desire to experience the thrill of things unknowable.* To do this the *teacher himself must exemplify the virtues he would inculcate.* Good teachers are mighty men and women of mental valor who burn with a flame that gives both heat and light.

3. *Is patient.* Patient with the stumbling of the uninitiated and also with the willingness to understand the naturalness of this stumbling. Patience also welcomes rational opposition and spirited critical dissent. It is accompanied by humility when the student asks the embarrassing or that which the teacher cannot answer.

4. *Possesses the ability to organize material.*
   a. Minute preparation of lecture, being careful this year's material is presented differently from last year's.
   b. Planning presentation along lines of major problems at hand—involves a planned survey of subject matter and issues, and acquaintance with material having a bearing on the subject under discussion.
   c. Weaving together the matter presented with that brought out in class discussion.

5. *Must be intellectually alive in the classroom.* Enthusiasm must be characteristic of his teaching. The source of freshness is love of teaching which communicates knowledge so that the student is led to make an old discovery as if it were new. It is perhaps important to know educational psychology, memory curves, and laws of learning, *but it is more important to love people and to know his students as individuals.*

6. *Must have an imaginative sympathy for the needs of the individual student.* He must do this without sacrificing

his own dignity, for the teacher who becomes the "pal" loses more than he gains. Sympathy is a positive attitude of imaginative concern with another's needs. In a teacher this is to see the potential in every student and bring that forth, often in spite of the student.

7. *Must possess vision.* The teacher must know where he is going and why, as this is the source of his professional spirit, his love of teaching, his enthusiasm.

8. *Must love teaching.* William Lyon Phelps, one of Yale's most beloved and most inspirational teachers, said, "*I do not know that I could make entirely clear to outsiders the pleasure I have in teaching. In my mind, teaching is not merely a lifework, a profession, an occupation, a struggle; it is a passion. I love to teach. I love to teach as a painter loves to paint, as a musician loves to play, as a singer loves to sing.*"

All of these qualities are important. But perhaps transcending all of them is the last—*a love of teaching.* To possess that quality is a deciding factor in a person's whole outlook. *It actually keeps a person young!* Young in heart, young in spirit; to an extent, even young physically. Frederick Jackson Turner, a historian at the University of Wisconsin, is an example of what we mean. One incident concerning the beloved pedagogue, recounted by Carl Lotus Becker, is particularly enlightening.

"On the faculty of that university [Wisconsin]," Mr. Becker wrote, "there was a man whom a young lawyer in my town referred to as 'Old Freddie Turner.'

"'Is he old?' I asked, picturing the long gray locks of a Faust before the devil comes in the spotlight.

"'Oh no, not *old*. We just called him that, I don't know why—just a rough way of showing boyish admiration without being sentimental about it, I suppose.'

"'What does he teach?'

"'Well, he teaches American history. *But it's not what he teaches*—the subject, I mean. The subject doesn't matter. *It's what he is*, the personality and all that sort of thing. *It's some-*

thing he gives you—inspiration, new ideas, a fresh light on things in general. It's something he makes you want to do or be.'"

THERE'S REASON ENOUGH

The *motives* which should impel the Christopher-minded man or woman to take up a teaching career go hand in hand with the *qualities* which a good teacher should possess. To a degree, these motives are synonymous with the qualities desired. One teacher who has been long in the field and knows whereof she speaks has set down the following motives, which she considers most important.

1. Because teaching offers the opportunity to influence others to become *whole men* as does no other field.
2. Because teaching, regardless of field, may *develop* in the student the prime *ability to think.*
3. Because the teacher can, through the medium of any subject matter, *inculcate right moral principles.*
4. Because the teacher may *inspire others to seek for knowledge.*
5. Because the teacher may become a *direct influence upon his students and those he meets* in a way offered to him in few other fields today.
6. Because the professor has *more chance* within his field for *individual research, continued study,* and *development of his creative ability.*
7. Because the teacher often has a personal teacher-student relationship that is enriching to both.
8. Because the environmental conditions of most university and college libraries, laboratories, et cetera, are good and often excellent.
9. Because the *companionship of other teachers* of his institution is *enriching* and stimulating.
10. Because the *environment* within the small college or university, which is usually in a small town, is *extremely fine for the raising of his family.*
11. Because the college or university can *offer him security*

which as a scholar is important in his own development
and enrichment.

ADMINISTRATIVE POSTS

Not all positions in the field of education are directly involved with teaching in the classroom. There are a number of
important *administrative posts* also. When planning and preparing for a teaching career, these posts should be considered
as objectives at which to aim. The opportunity to achieve
them will not always be present, of course. But they have to
be filled by someone—and the more sound-thinking, competent
men and women in the educational field there are who seek
them, the better off our entire educational system will be.

To avoid the pitfalls which any profession has for those
whose duties require the supervision of others, the following
points of comparison should prove helpful. The material
listed is taken from the textbook, *Introduction to Education*
by Lester D. and Alice Crow.

THE AUTOCRATIC ADMINISTRATOR	THE DEMOCRATIC ADMINISTRATOR
1. Thinks he can sit by himself and see all angles of a problem.	1. Realizes the potential power in thirty or fifty brains.
2. Does not know how to use the experience of others.	2. Knows how to utilize that power.
3. Cannot bear to let any of the strings of management slip from his fingers.	3. Knows how to delegate duties.
4. Is so tied to routine details that he seldom tackles his larger job.	4. Frees himself from routine details in order to turn his energy to creative leadership.
5. Is jealous of ideas . . . when someone else makes a proposal.	5. Is quick to recognize and praise an idea that comes from someone else.

THE AUTOCRATIC ADMINISTRATOR	THE DEMOCRATIC ADMINISTRATOR
6. Makes decisions that should have been made by the group.	6. Refers to the group all matters that concern the group.
7. Adopts a paternalistic attitude toward the group: "I know best."	7. Maintains the position of friendly, helpful adviser both on personal and professional matters.
8. Expects hero-worship, giggles of delight at his attempts at humor, and so forth.	8. Wishes to be respected as a fair and just individual, as he respects others.
9. Does not admit even to himself that he is autocratic.	9. Consciously practices democratic techniques.
10. Sacrifices everything—teachers, students, progress—to the end of a smooth-running system.	10. Is more concerned with the growth of individuals involved than with freedom from annoyances.
11. Is greedy for publicity.	11. Pushes others into the foreground so that they may taste success.
12. Gives to others as few opportunities for leadership as possible. Makes committee assignments, then outlines all duties and performs many of them himself.	12. Believes that as many individuals as possible should have opportunities to take responsibility and exercise leadership.

MORE THAN TEACHERS, MORE THAN ADMINISTRATORS

The qualities and motives listed previously for teachers apply, of course, to administrators as well. Moreover, the teacher or administrator whose objective is to bring to millions of young people the consciousness of Him Who is the Way, the Truth, and the Life must realize that he or she is more than just an instructor, more than just a supervisor. His or her relationship to the students should go much deeper than that. The students themselves are aware of this. As two of them commented not long ago:

"We no longer look upon our instructors as cold and distant pedagogues; we turn to them for guidance not only in problems immediately relating to school, but also for personal counsel. These talks constitute a most valuable part of our education. . . ."

What these pupils said is but another way of phrasing what one man, Charles Edward Gatman of Amherst College, called by William James the greatest teacher in the United States, said of the average teacher's responsibility and opportunity: *"The moral excellence, the personal loveliness of the pupil is the true crown of glory of a teacher.* As well instruct a brute as a child, if the beauty of manhood or womanhood does not unfold, if no ambition, no aspiration after a noble life is awakened, if there are no bright dreams of the future. It has long been known that certain plastic substances brought in contact with mother-of-pearl and allowed time to harden will take on its variegated splendor. *To impress oneself thus on an immortal being—an impression time can never efface— may well excite the envy of the angels in Heaven. It is immortality."*

4.

How to Become a College Teacher

A junior at Yale who plans to take up college teaching as a life's work told us that it was the Christopher emphasis on "taking a job with a purpose" that started him thinking in the direction of the educational field while he was still a college freshman.

When a friend asked him why he picked this particular field, he replied very simply, but very much to the point: "Somebody has to teach the ones who are coming up. Others have put a lot of time and energy on me, and this is one way I can repay them." Then he added:

"But I think of teaching as something more than a cold duty. As I see it, teaching is about the closest thing to the religious life. It gives you a chance to play a part in passing on to others the great old truths that have come down to us. When I have finished the thirty or forty years ahead that have to be spent doing something, I'd like to look back on them as years of helping others, not simply of helping myself."

Ordinarily, teachers' training schools and colleges, normal schools, schools of education, and liberal-arts colleges graduate their students with a bachelor's degree, or a normal-school certificate qualifying them to teach in the elementary or secondary schools.

But training teachers to instruct in our colleges and universities is something else again, since, by and large, there are no schools specifically designed to train them for that purpose. Most college professors of academic subjects are college graduates who have continued their studies in graduate schools, taken their higher degrees, and finally have received their doctorate.

Of course it is quite possible that the man or woman with only a bachelor's degree may be engaged as lecturer or instructor, but advancement to the higher grade of assistant professor, associate professor, and full professor is rarely accorded except to those holding higher degrees.

The director of the placement bureau of one of the most well-known colleges in the East gave this summary of the qualifications and opportunities:

1. B.A. degree: No chance in large university; small chance in small college.

2. M.A. degree: No chance in large university; slight chance in average-sized college; *best opportunity in small college.*

3. Ph.D.: Good opportunity in medium-sized college; very

good in small college; possible in university if applicant's work is personally known.

4. Ph.D., plus publications, plus experience: Good chance in university.

ROUTES TO COLLEGE TEACHING

Strictly speaking, there are three major routes to a college teaching career:

I. THROUGH GRADUATE STUDY.

a. Teaching a section in a large university.

b. Reading for a professor and counseling students in a large college or university.

c. Possibly teaching a class in a very small college.

Note: College students of exceptional ability frequently have the opportunity of applying for and receiving scholarships or fellowships to aid them to graduate work in their chosen field. Participation in such benefits entails full-time devotion to study, research, and some administrative duties. Most full-time graduate students, whether on scholarship or on their own, can complete the work of the doctorate in *three* to *four* years.

Part-time graduate students are, for the most part, men and women who are teaching in elementary and secondary school and have no thought of taking up college work. Others are college teachers who are continuing study for higher degrees. And, occasionally, exceptional students, especially those in smaller colleges which do not have graduate-school facilities, are offered teaching positions as instructors on a part-time or full-time basis in their own institutions.

For men and women such as these, however, there is a very great obligation to perfect their skills so that they may better fulfill their duties to the students who come under their care and who have a right to expect the best instruction possible.

II. THROUGH EDUCATIONAL TRAINING INSTITUTIONS.

These institutions are rare for the college-teaching level, for most schools of education train for elementary or secondary level. The very large institutions give limited courses in teaching techniques for junior college and the regular college approach.

III. FROM THE RANKS OF THE PROFESSIONS.

Very often doctors, lawyers, social-service workers, engineers, writers, and artists combine their professional activities with teaching; occasionally they may even give up their private pursuits for full-time teaching careers.

DON'T NEGLECT THESE

To help those who are interested in making the instruction of our youth their goal in life, we suggest that there are several ways of going about the *actual process of getting a teaching job*. The task of finding a position can be broken down as follows:

A. Making application through university placement bureaus.

B. Making application through state and federal placement bureaus.

C. Contacting the school in which a person has studied. This method is fairly successful for those who have been outstanding students.

D. Contacting strategically located friends or colleagues.

Sometimes these strategically located friends or colleagues in or allied to the teaching profession have contacts that can be utilized. Then, too, *commercial teachers' agencies* are frequently consulted by the large universities, as well as by smaller colleges, when vacancies arise. The offices of these agencies are state-licensed, and the better-known ones are well-organized, well-informed, and quite efficient. The candidate should register with one or more of these agencies and keep in touch with them at regular intervals. Promptness in replying to requests for references, experience, et cetera, is a courtesy upon which special emphasis should be laid, for the very good reason that it is a determining factor in any estimate of an applicant's fitness for a teaching position.

KEY SPOTS AND ACTIVITIES

Once you have made up your mind to become a teacher, and once you have taken into consideration the information we have listed in these pages, there are a few additional points you should bear in mind.

In the teaching profession there are important posts to be filled on various committees within a college or university, posts where a Christopher-minded teacher will be in a strong position to influence both students and faculty alike. *Book committees,* for example, in various departments of the college pass upon texts to be used by students. This function obviously is of great strategic importance and is ideal for the influence of Christopher action.

Right now the teacher who has a purpose to change the world for the better should begin to prepare himself or herself to seek a post on such textbook committees, and should earn the appointment by virtue of superior knowledge, unstinting effort, and perseverance. And once on such committees, he or she should work for the appointment of other instructors of high principles and sound values in the teaching profession.

FRIENDLY ADVISER

Another important post in college work is that of *faculty adviser* or *counselor.* A post such as faculty adviser or counselor presents a golden opportunity for Christopher action, for action by those teachers who see in each of their fellow men the image and likeness of their Creator. Here the Christopher can obey the Christian injunction to *"instruct the ignorant"* and to *"counsel the doubtful."* By even such a small thing as a word of caution to some student in regard to his choice of a course which cleverly conceals its real aim of undermining American democratic principles or the Christian code of morality, the faculty adviser or counselor can put forth positive action for *good.*

Then, again, the counselor's aid may be used in resolving

difficulties between instructors and students. Sometimes this aid will take the form of direct intervention; at other times that of intelligent advice.

FULL-TIME JOBS

Teachers who act as *vocational counselors* frequently put in full time at that work. Theirs is a great opportunity to shape the immediate—and perhaps the remote—future of a young man or woman. Since choice of a life's career is of paramount importance to the young person of sound values, whatever influence the teacher can exert will do far-reaching good. *This is guidance for life;* this is helping shape a career with a purpose beyond the mere aim of earning a living; this is molding, so to speak, the aspirations of our youth so as better to reflect the glory of God into the lives of as many of His children as possible.

FURTHER ACTIVITIES

By reason of his talents, the breadth of his culture, and his many other advantages, the teacher has duties and moral obligations other than those already listed. Among the most serious of these is the requirement that he become an integral part of his community, whether that community be large or small.

Participation in activities which combine scholastic and civic aspects is one means of making a profound effect on the life of the community.

These activities may take the form of veterans' groups, welfare organizations, civic-advancement leagues, voters' leagues, health administration, public-work associations, parent-teacher federations, and many others. In many cases these groups do serve now—and have served in the past—as sounding boards for subversive speakers and lecturers. The teacher participating in these organizations should make it his business to know the character and reputation of speakers. He should be on his guard, too, for local "fellow travelers" who find membership in these groups a convenient opportunity for projecting themselves further into their activities. The teacher must be alert to get himself into a position where he can block the engagement of speakers of known subversive tendencies or where he can refute such pronouncements as may already have been made.

Finally, not only as a teacher but as a citizen as well, the Christopher can make himself heard and heeded in places where his opinion counts by communicating with his elected representatives in the local government, state legislature, and Congress. Before these bodies there are always measures which affect, directly or indirectly, the well-being of the college and the teacher, both in a professional and civic sense.

The teacher in college, then, must complement his work as an instructor by participation in such other activities as his time, energies, and talents may permit, in an effort to *"reach out both hands in constant helpfulness to his fellow man."* He will fall short of that goal only to the extent that his vision carries him no farther than the mere academic progress of the students under his care. The teacher must aid in integrating academic proficiency with that *"proper sense of moral values"* without which education is aimless and futile.

With a clear realization of his role in bringing Christ into the classroom through his own well-defined sense of dedication. the Christopher-minded teacher will render a service that will last for time and for eternity.

As St. John Chrysostom put it fifteen hundred years ago: "What is nobler than to rule minds or to mold the character of the young? I consider that he who knows how to form the youthful mind is truly greater than any painter or sculptor."

FOR ADDITIONAL READING

CASTIELLO, J. *A Humane Psychology of Education*. New York: Sheed and Ward, 1936. Preface by Louis J. A. Mercier. Pp. xxiii + 254.

FLEXNER, ABRAHAM. *Universities, American, English, German.* New York: Oxford University Press, 1930.

KANE, W. A. *History of Education*. Chicago: Loyola University Press, 1935.

LAPP, JOHN A., and others. *Career as a College Professor*. Chicago: The Institute for Research, 1947.

THWING, CHARLES FRANKLIN. *The American College and University*. New York: Macmillan, 1935. P. 244.

WILSON, LOGAN. *The Academic Man*. New York: Oxford University Press, 1942. Pp. vi + 248.

VITALIZING LABOR RELATIONS

1.

A Study in Contrasts

Two years ago, in France, I talked with a group of dock workers whose plight was anything but a happy one. Their cheeks were sunken with hunger, their clothes in tatters. The most that any of them could earn in a week, I learned, was nine dollars—and there were many weeks in which they were without any work at all.

It might have been expected that they would be bitter at their lot, but they were not. Their only complaint was *that no one cared much about them*—no one showed any interest in helping them better their condition. They were forgotten men as far as government was concerned, they said. Businessmen were too engrossed in their own affairs to bother about them. Students talked a lot about doing something to correct the situation, but actually did little. Religious people showed only a token interest in championing their cause. "The only ones who even come to us are the Communists," one young man observed. "But we don't want them. They aren't really interested in helping us. All they want to do is to use us to climb to power."

The plight of workers in other countries is similarly bad. Will Lissner, economist of the New York *Times*, reported from Costa Rica, June 25, 1950, that "bumper crops of coffee at good prices are bringing a measure of prosperity today to most of the six republics of Central America. But most of the workers will get little or no benefit from it." Lissner pointed out that the majority of the people live on a "marginal existence . . . and though they are right on the continent of North America, within four hours' flying time of the most advanced industrial economy in the world, they have large sections where the invention of the wheel has made no impact."

Touching on another country in Central America, Lissner stated that prices in Guatemala are the highest in that area, with some imported goods costing two or three times the selling price in New York. The average carpenter gets one dollar a day, a street sweeper eighty cents, and the average common laborer in government public-works projects gets sixty-four cents a day.

Concluding his illuminating article, in which he showed how "living conditions sap the vitality and ambition of the laborer," Lissner sounded this hopeful and challenging note: "He [the worker], like the other folk of Central America, bears his poverty with patience and with dignity. But he yearns for a better life; the big ambition of his life is to share in some part of the blessings that he has heard North Americans enjoy without stint. He looks northward without envy but with hope."

Conditions for the laborer in much of the rest of the world, especially in Asia, where over half of humanity lives, are far worse than those in France and Latin America. To be at least acquainted with such conditions is desirable for these three important reasons:

1. They focus attention on the tremendous advance made by labor in the United States, with the consequent advantage to the home, the church, government, business, and all the professions.

2. They should be constant reminders of the level to which we in this country may fall if we do not take every reasonable

precaution to perfect our own system and remove every possible social injustice.

3. They highlight the huge job to be done, in behalf of labor over the world, by *sound* leadership. As followers of Christ, we in America have a serious responsibility to all men as members, under God, of one human family. Failure to recognize this responsibility carries with it the terrible penalty of recurring and devastating wars, followed, of course, by a state of economic chaos.

OUR GOAL

We do not pretend to speak with authority on economic problems. But we do hope that we may render a service nevertheless.

Our goal is to encourage persons with Christlike motives to enter the three great divisions of labor relations: (1) trade unions, (2) management, and (3) government. Furthermore, it is our hope to rekindle in those now occupying official posts in these spheres a determination to formulate and pursue at all times and under all circumstances policies that are fair to all parties concerned.

As in every other phase of the Christopher approach, the underlying motivation of each careerist must be basically *spiritual*. The importance of this was stressed not long ago by Pius XII when he said: *"The extent to which the representatives of labor are penetrated with the principles of the Gospel will decide in large measure the extent to which the society of tomorrow will be Christian."*

The Christopher contribution to the achievement of a truly Christian society can have far-reaching effects. Only recently we heard that our constantly repeated plea to union members to attend all union meetings was having more worth-while results than we had dared hope. An official of a leftist union stated flatly that the one group which was giving them the most trouble over the country was the Christopher movement, because it was getting more and more rank-and-file workers to attend union meetings regularly.

OUR FUNCTION

The problem associated with labor relations is an intricate one. There are many sound approaches to a solution, approaches which we leave to those better equipped to propose and apply. In this brief treatment we limit ourselves to that guidance which has met with widespread approval on the part of both labor and management. The basic principles which we offer are found in the labor encyclicals whose soundness has been well summed up by a Protestant scholar, Dr. Philip Taft, chairman of the Department of Economics at Brown University and a specialist in the history of labor. Writing recently in the magazine *America,* he said:

> While the present generation faces the grim task of defending society and its traditions against corrosion from within and attack from without, the problems themselves are not new, and guidance on these questions can still be found by non-Catholics as well as Catholics in the papal encyclicals, *Rerum Novarum* and *Quadragesimo Anno.*
>
> Despite their age, these documents have a vitality and freshness absent in the many contemporary pronouncements on social issues. Not only do they accurately diagnose the economic maladies of our time, but the remedies prescribed have been found effective in the past and are sufficiently potent to be helpful in the future.

To Dr. Taft's commendation might be added that of many others, among them Professor Joseph A. Schumpeter of the Department of Economics, Harvard University. Speaking before a meeting of the American Economic Association at the Hotel Commodore in New York City on December 30, 1949 (just one week before his death), Professor Schumpeter advocated that economists study the social encyclicals. This internationally renowned scholar deplored the fact that too few know these documents.

BEAR THESE IN MIND

Despite the necessary brevity of our presentation on the subject of career work in the labor field, it seems most important to include at least a few reminders from both of these encyclicals, which point out the obligations of labor, capital, and government. These reminders, briefly presented as they are, should nevertheless offer a sound basis of judgment in regard to a Christopher-minded person's course of action in the labor-relations field.

1. FOR THE GOOD OF ALL. "Wealth must be so distributed among the various individuals and classes of society that the common good of all, of which Leo XIII spoke, is thereby promoted. In other words, the good of the whole community must be safeguarded.

"By these principles of social justice one class is forbidden to exclude the other from a share in the profits. This sacred law is violated by an irresponsible wealthy class claiming everything and leaving the worker nothing; it is violated also by a propertyless wage-earning class who demand all the fruits of production as being the work of their hands.

"Each class then must receive its just share, and the distribution of wealth must be brought into conformity with the common good and social justice. The evil of modern society consists in the vast differences between the few who hold excessive wealth and the many who live in destitution." (*Quadragesimo Anno*)

2. LEFT TO US. "*The defining of private possessions has been left by God to man's industry and the laws of individual peoples.*" (*Rerum Novarum*)

3. ALL HAVE RIGHTS. "The earth, even though apportioned among private owners, ceases not by that fact to minister to the needs of all." (*Rerum Novarum*)

4. FAIR DISTRIBUTION. "*Every effort must be made that a just share only of the fruits of production be permitted to accumulate in the hands of the wealthy, and that an ample sufficiency be supplied to the workers.*" (*Quadragesimo Anno*)

5. **PENALTY OF INDIFFERENCE.** "We witness with sorrow the heedlessness of those who seem to make light of these imminent dangers and with stolid indifference allow the widespread propagation of those doctrines which seek by violence and bloodshed the destruction of all society. We condemn even more severely the foolhardiness of those who neglect to remove or modify such conditions as exasperate the minds of the people, and so prepare the way for the overthrow and ruin of the social order." (*Quadragesimo Anno*)

6. **THE ROLE OF GOVERNMENT.** *"Rights must be religiously respected wherever they are found; and it is the duty of Government to prevent and punish injury, and to protect each one in the possession of his own."* (*Rerum Novarum*)

7. **OBLIGATION OF LABOR.** "They [laborers] are to carry out *honestly* and *well* all equitable agreements freely made; they are not to injure Capital nor to outrage the person of the employer; they are never to employ violence in furthering their aims and they are to have nothing to do with men of evil principles." (*Rerum Novarum*)

8. **ABUSES TO BE AVOIDED.** *"While all men may justly strive to better their conditions, neither justice nor the common good allows any individual to seize the property of another, to lay violent hands thereon. While the vast number of workers prefer to better themselves by honest means, there are some who are guided by vicious principles. Their main purpose is to rouse their fellows to disorder, violence, and revolution. Government should intervene to restrain such firebrands, to save the workers from being led astray; and to protect lawful owners from spoilation."* (*Rerum Novarum*)

9. **EXCESSES OF COMMUNISM.** "Communism teaches and pursues a twofold aim: merciless class warfare and abolition of private property. And it does this not in secret and by hidden methods, but openly and by every means, even the most violent. To obtain these ends Communists shrink from nothing. And once they have attained power, it is incredible, indeed it seems portentous, how cruel and inhuman they show themselves to be." (*Quadragesimo Anno*)

10. CLASS HARMONY. The great mistake of the Communists is *"to have . . . the idea that class is naturally hostile to class; that rich and poor are intended by nature to live at war with one another. So irrational and so false is this view that the exact contrary is the truth.*

"Just as the symmetry of the human body is the result of the disposition of the members of the body, so in a State it is ordained by nature that these two classes should exist in harmony and agreement, and should, as it were, fit into one another, so as to maintain the equilibrium of the body politic. Each requires the other; capital cannot do without labor, nor labor without capital." (*Rerum Novarum*)

11. ALSO RIGHTS. "In all contracts between employers and workers there is always the condition, expressed or understood, that there be allowed proper rest for soul and body. To agree in any other sense would be against what is right and just. For it never can be right or just to require on the one side, or to promise on the other, the giving up of those duties which a man owes to his God and to himself." (*Rerum Novarum*)

The Christopher-minded careerist in the labor-relations field can do much to change the whole world for the better by putting these and the other sound principles of the encyclicals into everyday practice.

2.

There's a Job for You

For those who contemplate a career in labor, the story of Pete Belmonte sums up completely the motives which Christopher-minded men and women in this vital field should possess.

Pete Belmonte was a paper cutter by trade. In the shop where he was employed there were some two hundred-odd **workmen**, illiterate for the most part, and Pete promptly took it upon himself to make their problems his personal concern. Soon he was elected shop steward, and to fit himself for his new duties he enrolled at a labor school, where he took up the study of parliamentary law, labor law, how to handle grievances, et cetera. He learned methods of organization and labor ethics.

As time went by and his worth became more and more recognized, he was offered the managership of the plant—an unusual procedure, to say the least. He turned the offer down. He said he could not abandon the two hundred-odd workers who looked up to him as their protector. Shortly afterward he received another offer, this time a highly paid position in a liquor concern. Again he turned down the job. This, in his own words, was his reaction: *"When I die and St. Peter is introducing me to the good Lord, I'd much rather hear him say, 'Lord, here is Pete, the paper worker,' instead of 'Lord, this is Peter Belmonte, the rich liquor salesman.'"*

When the union offered him a job as business agent, however, he accepted, even though it meant earning quite a bit less a week than he was getting. He was willing to make the sacrifice because he felt the position offered more of a chance to help his fellow workmen.

Not long ago Pete died from a sudden heart attack brought on by overwork. But his good influence didn't die with him. His example has inspired others to step in and take up where he left off. Here, indeed, was a real Christopher who so lived his beliefs that he literally laid down his life for his fellow men.

UNIONS TODAY

In this country today there are over fifteen million union members who belong to some sixty thousand locals. These locals, in turn, are members of one hundred and ninety national unions. All of these are associated with one of two great labor federations. Two thirds of all those engaged in manufacturing industry work under union contracts.

In the forefront of organized labor, it has been estimated,

there are at least one hundred thousand labor leaders or officials in union membership. To a considerable degree, the destiny of our nation is in their hands, yet their potential for good or evil is out of proportion to their numbers. Golden and Ruttenburg, in their book, *The Dynamics of Industrial Democracy,* see this quite clearly when they write: "To serve such dynamic ends unions need constructive and unselfish leadership. . . . There are many outstanding leaders of organized labor and management, to be sure, that fill these requirements, but there are not enough of them and, further, too many of them are past the age of fifty."

One of the largest and most progressive unions in the country has taken steps to solve this problem. It has established, on an experimental basis, a *training institute* to train prospective union officers of the future. As one top official of this organization told us: "*Perhaps more than any other field, we need specially trained people. There is no such thing as just being 'in' the labor movement, or in any labor job. Each job is a different type and requires certain personality traits and educational background, plus desire and interest. . . .*"

For those who have a Christopher purpose in their desire to enter the vital field of labor, we are submitting a listing which should give a fairly good idea of the various opportunities and job possibilities. Differences, of course, exist from union to union as to the nature and the name of any particular job. Often the person holding one job performs the functions of many other jobs. Then, again, several jobs are sometimes compressed into one. Also, some jobs are salaried and some jobs are not.

CHART OF JOBS IN THE UNION FIELD

A. *The Local Level*
  1. The Executive Board
    a. Officers and Committees
  2. Staff Positions
    a. Shop Steward
    b. Business Agent
    c. Counselor

B. *State or Regional Level*
  1. The Executive Board
    a. Officers and Committees

2. Staff Positions
   a. Research Director
   b. Educational Director
   c. Public Relations
3. Metropolitan or County Federation
   a. Officers and Committees

C. *National (or International) Level*
   1. Executive Board
      a. Officers and Committees
   2. Staff Positions
      a. (Same as for state, cf. above)
   3. State or District Council or Federation
      a. Officers and Committees

D *National Federation or Congress*
   1. Officers and Committees
   2. State or Regional Council
   3. City Centrals (These all include the same staff positions and services as above)

E. *On All Levels*
   1. Newspapers and News Service
   2. Organizer, Editor, et cetera
   3. Legal Service
      a. Lawyers
      b. Legal Research Services

COLLEGE GRADUATES WANTED

The day when only laborers could take a union job is gone. As is apparent from the above chart, the openings for specialists with college background are numerous. It is possible, therefore, to divide union jobs into two general classifications: (1) the administrative jobs held by union members, and (2) the jobs in research, law, analysis of problems peculiar to labor, and others of a similar nature, which are generally filled by college men.

Any student who enters college with his sights set on preparing himself for a job as a labor-relations expert in unions should emphasize such studies as economics, statistics, labor law, history, structure of unions, and writing. After graduation, labor experience will prove invaluable. A couple of years at the bench, plus a union card, should help him reach his goal more easily.

One college graduate we know started out as an economics instructor in a metropolitan high school. However, his desire to get *directly* into the labor field was so strong that he set out to establish as many union contacts as he could. He taught in a labor school part time and gave lectures to workers' groups. At this writing he is a full-time research director for a large union in New York. He made up for his lack of experience in the field by his part-time work in labor circles.

Another college graduate who is at present educational director of a large textile union also advanced to his position the hard way. After finishing college he got a job in the clothing industry. While there he did part-time work on a union magazine. This experience, together with his college training, proved excellent recommendation for his present job.

A young journalism student took a job soon after graduation as editorial secretary on a union publication. Now, some four years later, he is in complete charge of the rewrite desk.

BACKBONE OF UNION LABOR RELATIONS

The strength of unions, however, still rests in the administrative posts, in the officers, staffs, officials, and committees. There is only one way to reach these positions—*by coming up through the ranks*. It is on the floor of the plant or factory that the valuable experience of dealing with people is acquired. Then will come membership on some union committee, a job in the lower ranks of union management, and so on.

SIMPLE RULES

For all who seek a job in labor-relations work on *any* level, however, we offer the following simple rules:

1. Be active in union affairs. Attend all meetings and make yourself heard.

2. Know the workers and be interested in them.

3. Volunteer for spare-time jobs—and do the work!

4. Learn all you can about union organizations and policies. Include parliamentary procedure and public speaking in your schedule.

5. Read a number of trade-union publications to gain a grounding in labor problems.

6. As soon as possible, aim for an influential union job or post to serve as a goal for reasonable advancement.

KEY SPOTS

All of the one hundred thousand jobs held by union officials are posts of influence, since they affect some fifteen million union members. Here we point out a certain few of these jobs which wield greater influence than most of the others.

The *union officer* on the national or local level occupies a vital spot. General policies, grievances, negotiation, or agreements are among his duties. The top influential offices are *president, secretary-treasurer,* and *executive board member.* These are elective offices. Consequently, the closer one adheres to the five rules laid down for advancement, which are listed above, the better one's chances to find a place on the union ballot.

On the local level, the *business agent* is a pivotal figure. In some unions he is the handy man with a multitude of important chores. The job, also an elective one, requires initiative, a sense of responsibility, and union experience.

On *all* levels there are essential jobs in *writing* and *public relations.* The *editorial department* deals with union publications, pamphlets, and notices. In the United States there are one hundred forty-two union publications in addition to the national publications of the two major labor federations. The department of *public relations* in the larger unions shares with the editorial staff great power for good, constructive labor relations.

The *educational director* is usually on the national level and is concerned with worker education. His policies can spell benefit or harm for the union and for the community. To qualify for this post considerable experience in union-training programs is required.

On the local level, an important labor-relations post exists in conjunction with the work of the plant. The post is that of *shop steward*. He is elected to the post by the workers, and among his functions are those concerned with receiving grievances, forwarding complaints to the union officials, and transmitting instructions from those officials to the rank and file of the union membership. He conciliates if he can. If this is not possible, he processes the complaint and sends it on to higher authority. The shop steward must be skilled in human relations and familiar with labor problems and policies. All in all, it is perhaps the best source of experience for a labor-relations career in any capacity.

OPPORTUNITIES FOR WOMEN

Over three million women are now members of organized labor. Their place and importance in union work and labor relations are growing steadily. In theory, no job in unions is closed to the female applicant. From a practical standpoint this is likewise true, provided she can meet the requirements demanded for a particular post. The feminine influence, moreover, could very well be what is needed in this field today to soften the rough spots and establish permanent labor peace.

One woman who is secretary to the president of one of the country's outstanding unions says that she grew up in an atmosphere of constant struggle between labor and management. She worked in private industry for a while and then, determined to do her bit to improve conditions, she shifted to the labor field, where she felt her influence for good could be put to better use.

In her secretarial post she is in charge of the complete schedule of the union president's office. She acts in a liaison capacity for her boss with all the departments. In addition she takes care of the many individual relief and social-service cases which constantly stream into the general offices of the union. Her interest in labor is as sincere as it is apparently inexhaustible, and her interest has had a beneficial influence on members of her own family.

Of her three brothers, one is teaching labor in the school system of the community; another is research director and editor of a union paper; the third is in industry, concentrating on labor law.

THE RANK AND FILE

Each member of a union, male or female, can wield an influence for good far greater than he or she may realize. This can be accomplished if he or she will do two things: (1) take an interest in the affairs of the union to which he or she belongs; and (2) become active personally in union activities—run for office, work on official business, take responsibility, especially in those jobs which no one wants.

Bad labor leadership of all sorts is ultimately the result of an inactive, inarticulate union membership, and the influential posts are often let go by default. Too many union members fail to take any part or interest whatsoever in union affairs.

One does not stand to gain much financially by taking an active part in union matters. That much should be fairly obvious, especially if a person is Christopher-minded. "But," as one labor leader pointed out, "those who are working in behalf of labor are expected to take a certain amount of remuneration in dividends of social conscience. It will never buy you a yacht . . . but you'll be sleeping awfully well."

3.

Management's Role in Labor Relations

On July 19, 1950, at a conference on "human relations in industry" held at Silver Bay, Lake George, New York, Walter H. Wheeler, Jr., president of Pitney-Bowes, Incorporated, of

Stamford, Connecticut, made these significant observations:

"It takes an underlying faith in the spiritual nature of man, in his divine right to the dignity of individuality, and in his struggle, often in spite of his own perversity, to achieve a nobler life. Such faith generally stems from religion. . . . No organization of society—whether it be a nation or an industrial plant —can succeed which sacrifices this fundamental on the altar of materialism . . . what many of us overlook entirely is that when we attempt to run our industries and deal with industrial relations solely on a basis of materialism, we make the same fundamental mistake as the Communists, however unorthodox it sounds to try to mix man's spiritual needs with profit and loss. . . ."

HUMAN RELATIONS

Industrial relations have been defined as a sort of "human engineering" in industry, a way of life. Industrial relations are human relations. The aim of work in this field is to promote the smooth and efficient operation of the economic system with due consideration for honesty and justice toward all concerned. Industrial or labor-relations work deals mainly with the following activities: (1) employment, i.e., hiring, firing, and training of men; (2) negotiation and administration of agreements; (3) arbitrating and conciliating differences; (4) applying labor legislation. Industrial or labor relations are based—or should be based—on nothing more than respect for each and every individual as a human being made in the image and likeness of God. For management to treat workers simply as cogs in a machine and deny them recognition as individual human personalities is to court disaster. *Forbes Magazine of Business* quotes a midwestern mechanic who makes this point very emphatically. *"The only opportunity that a man wants,"* the mechanic said, *"is the opportunity to be treated as a dignified human being, like the boss is treated."*

Heartening testimony that management is coming to appreciate this fact is contained in what one official of an industrial concern, the *Murray Manufacturing Corporation* of Brooklyn,

New York, had to say regarding the necessity of developing good human relations with employees. *"Many people in industrial relations feel that their whole job centers around the Union's contract. This is probably because nearly everything we do must be done in relation to the framework and limitations set up by a collective-bargaining agreement. It seems to me, however, that if we are to do more than our day-to-day job and attempt to do the task before us as Christ means us to do it, we cannot think of the Union contract and decide that if we have lived up to our legal obligations we are doing all that is required of us. More is demanded of us than a simple living up to the letter of the law."*

THE NEED HAS GROWN

Not so very long ago all labor relations in management were taken care of exclusively by the owner or the boss of a company. He was in immediate contact with his employees and mixed labor relations with the job itself. Today, however, business and industry have grown into such sprawling plants and giant corporations that the problem of employer-employee relations has become considerably more complex.

In industry it has become a separate, *specialized* part of general management. In a company of any appreciable size an expert or director takes care of it. In the larger plants whole departments are devoted to it. Today an industrial-relations man may be anyone from the vice-president of a company or corporation, who negotiates directly with a union, to some minor official. Or he may be a person who is in charge of *all* labor relations and has authority to settle all grievances. He might be a public-relations man who acts as liaison between the union and the company. In the latter event some official of the company undoubtedly would work with him. But labor relations in any firm will be satisfactory to all concerned only in proportion as every executive in management shows a personal interest in personnel responsibility.

A group of thirty-eight business executives whose primary

responsibility is labor relations (and who rate among the top men in their field in America) were asked to list the qualifications they believed men entering the field ought to have. In the recent survey, conducted by *Business Week*, the industrial-relations men included:

1. *Academic Training:* A bachelor's degree was felt by most to be essential. Many said they would insist upon graduate training. Emphasis was placed upon training in psychology. About 50 per cent of these executives thought the person entering this field should have academic training in business. The other 50 per cent preferred the liberal arts and humanities. Few recommended academic training in industrial relations.

2. *Age Requirements:* The range here is from thirty to fifty-five years. Most of these executives preferred a forty- to forty-five-year-old man.

3. *Work Background:* The most important experience these men could have is *factory labor*. Next comes *experience in union negotiating, in personnel work, and in administration*.

4. *Outside Interests:* The labor-relations man ought to be, these executives felt, active in community and civic affairs. They should have political, cultural, and recreational interests, and they should actively participate in professional societies.

Asked, "What are the most useful sources of information which you find important in doing your job?" most of these men replied, ". . . personal contacts—with other business executives, with professionals in the labor-relations field, with employees and supervisors in their own company, and with union officials." Although many of them indicated that conference groups were useful, they stressed that off-the-record and informal meetings were especially valuable to them.

How broad the interests of a personnel man ought to be is indicated in the replies of these executives to a query on their reading. The subject in which most of them were interested is *psychology*. Sociology, economics, history, and philosophy got frequent mention. Some like literature, others prefer political science. One reads in the field of religion, another in poetry; but *only one* said he does *only* professional reading.

Management labor-relations officials must be understanding and judicious persons. Tact and a high sense of social justice are necessary equipment. But proportionate to their grave responsibility is their potential for good. All employees of a concern will gain or suffer by a wrong decision on their part, or an unjust policy, or a negative attitude where a positive approach is most needed.

A college background is usually essential for jobs other than those of plant foreman, although experience and self-training may qualify some individuals. Charles E. Wilson, president of the General Electric Company, is one example of a man who came up from the ranks. Mr. Wilson, who has just completed his fiftieth year with GE, started out at a three-dollar-a-week job with the Sprague Electric Company—which later became part of GE—soon after he finished the eighth grade (his father had died when Wilson was only three).

The day Wilson's wages reached eight dollars a week he told his mother she didn't have to work any longer and he took over as breadwinner. On the advice of William T. Ruete, the Sprague Company's general manager, to "look forward and equip yourself for your next job," Wilson went to night school, paying for his courses by tutoring pupils in mathematics and physics. In 1940 he became president of GE.

Always a religious man, Wilson has never lost touch with his youthful struggles nor with those of the men with whom he worked. *"A concern that places the cash register above human rights and human values deserves to go out of business,"* he said not long ago. And then he added this spiritual note which all of us might take to heart: *"What we need in America today, in fact in the entire world, is more men and women unashamed to pray."*

TYPES OF LABOR-RELATIONS JOBS IN MANAGEMENT

To give Christopher-minded persons who are interested in this phase of a particularly vital field some idea of the variety of jobs for which they may qualify, below is a listing which may prove of immediate value:

A. *Directory of Industrial Relations*
   1. Director of Research (Personnel and Statistics)
   2. Director of Labor Relations
   3. Administrator of Wages and Salaries

B. *Supervisory Personnel (Indirectly in Labor Relations)*
   1. Foreman or Supervisor
   2. Superintendent
   3. Plant Manager

KEY SPOTS

All of these jobs are important. However, there are certain key spots which wield greater influence than others. These posts are:

Industrial Relations Director. This is the top job in the field in any firm. It is highly specialized, requiring work in graduate schools with emphasis on industrial relations in all its phases. Several years of experience in personnel work and public relations are needed, plus good judgment, resourcefulness, and tact.

Director of Labor Relations. A person in this position has an over-all jurisdiction in labor problems and situations. A union business agent, for example, can aim for this spot provided he has the proper initiative, plus a familiarity with the company, the contracts, policies, and practices.

Director of Supervisory Training and *Counselor* are also key spots at which Christopher-minded men and women should aim, since they are influential in forming the mental habits of foremen and workers for good or evil. On-the-job training is usually sufficient experience to qualify a person for this type of position.

ALSO IMPORTANT

Within the personnel of management there are several jobs which, although primarily designed to serve a firm in maintaining high production, are nevertheless intimately related to labor-relations work. They are of critical importance.

The *foreman* or *supervisor* might well be thought of as the embodiment of all the policies and practices of management. He is the connecting link between the business concern and the individual worker. His attitude, his sense of justice and fairness are of utmost importance in promoting peaceful and constructive relations. He can rise from the ranks of his union to foreman. For this he requires ability in handling grievances and personal problems.

Superintendents and *Plant Managers,* while only indirectly concerned with labor relations, yet play an important role. They do much to shape labor policy. It is possible for a worker to come up from the ranks to obtain such a position; often it is by appointment from outside sources. Experience is the best teacher for this type of job.

SOMETHING TO REMEMBER

The above listing, brief as it is, does not, of course, give the complete picture of labor relations in the area of industry. But it should afford some idea of the variety of jobs and the special talents required. As time goes on, these jobs will assume an ever-increasing place in our national life. Robert W. Johnson, Chairman of the Board of Johnson & Johnson, in his book, *Or Forfeit Freedom,* states very clearly why this should be so.

> *The day has passed* [he wrote] *when business was a private matter—if it ever was. In a business society, every act of business has social consequences and may arouse public interest. Every time business hires, builds, sells, or buys, it is acting for the American people as well as for itself, and it must be prepared to accept full responsibility for its acts.*

In commenting on what we have referred to as the "human engineering" side of this vital field, Mr. Johnson made this pertinent observation:

Many people are surprised to learn that straight thinking on the human side of labor-management relations is so difficult to find. The business world has plenty of experts who can think through on merchandising problems, banking problems, engineering problems, and problems in other fields. All too often, however, the human—which means the social—problems either remain untouched or are left to outsiders whose ideas are then rejected as visionary. Meanwhile backlogs of confusion and misunderstanding pile up and develop into conflicts . . . the bulk of business lags behind advertising, which long ago discovered that people are human and hired psychologists to learn how to deal with customers. Business leaders must recognize the demand for a professional approach to labor-management relations. . . .

To Mr. Johnson's remarks we can add only a heartfelt "Amen."

4.

Labor Relations in Government

A few months ago a young man came into our office seeking advice as to just where he could begin in the field of labor relations. He had recently graduated from college, but he felt that his education had not prepared him for his hoped-for career, since his studies had been mainly in the "liberal arts." "I've no contacts or training for industrial relations or for union work," he added. "I want to get into the labor-relations field, but I don't know how to start."

This young man was surprised when it was pointed out to him that there was another phase of the labor sphere which offered innumerable opportunities to accomplish great good, provided he was willing to work hard and learn. The phase to which we referred was *government labor*.

Since unions and management have full-time problems of their own, and since the average citizen is far from a disinterested spectator of the labor scene, it is perfectly understandable that, *within reasonable limits,* government should step into the picture in order to safeguard the rights of all our people—*"to promote the general welfare,"* as it is phrased in the Constitution.

In general, the role of the government is: (1) to make and enforce just laws regulating employer-employee relations where the public interest is at stake; (2) to conciliate and arbitrate differences; (3) to prevent or bring to a close prolonged strikes or lockouts; and (4) to provide for the public safety.

Further, government labor work operates on *three levels:* (1) federal; (2) state; and (3) local. As a rule, the state and local operations are modeled on the federal, although on a smaller and somewhat simpler scale.

THE DEPARTMENT OF LABOR

This is one of the major departments of the federal government. In it vital decisions are made daily, affecting over sixty million of workers, employers, and consumers. Ten different bureaus, employing 4,971 people, comprise the department, including such important branches as the *Office of the Secretary of Labor,* the *Bureaus of Labor Standards, Labor Statistics, Employment Security,* and others. Most positions are headed by a staff official who may have from two to two hundred people working in his operation.

All states have a Department of Labor, or its equivalent, including some or all of the bureaus and branches of the federal government. The scope of their operations is determined by the size and industrial condition of the state.

One woman who holds a responsible post in the Labor Department took up government work not long after she had graduated from college in North Carolina. Her interest had always run along labor lines and, while still a student, she wrote a paper on the subject as her term thesis. To gather as much information as possible, she sent a letter to the Department of Labor in Washington, D.C. Her letter happened to fall into the hands of a member of the staff who always made it a point to answer inquiries with a personal note whenever she could, rather than just forward a pamphlet or some other piece of literature. This extra courtesy so impressed the young college student that when she graduated she wrote to her correspondent in Washington. "You sent such a friendly letter to me, showing a personal interest in what I was trying to do, that I am writing to tell you that I am applying for a position in the Labor Department as soon as I can get my affairs in order. I thought you'd like to be the first to know."

An encouraging note went back to this young lady, stating that she would not be able to take a professional job, as she was not yet ready for that, but that she might apply for a position as a typist. She took the advice and, while following her routine assignment, she studied in her spare time to fit herself for more advanced work. Today she is one of the most valued members of the department.

NATIONAL LABOR RELATIONS BOARD

Next in prominence to the Labor Department is the *National Labor Relations Board,* whose function is to administer the National Labor Relations Act. This agency has wide authority and discretionary power. Its principal aim is: (1) recognize legitimate unions, (2) to prevent discriminatory practices of employers or union, and (3) to hear complaints. The board is like a great impartial umpire who looks after the good of all concerned.

Some states have a "little" Labor Relations Act modeled on the federal act, and therefore they have labor boards similar to the federal board.

GOVERNMENT MEDIATION AND CONCILIATION SERVICES

These branches perform the difficult task of attempting, by means of *persuasion,* to prevent labor strife and keep the economic machine running smoothly. They can make recommendations but cannot make decisions for the parties involved. Conciliators and their staffs can do immense good. Of course they must be experts in human relations as well as in labor law and policies.

The role of the government mediator is now an integral part of the American labor scene. The law of the land, in fact, prescribes that the Mediation Service of federal and state governments be notified within thirty days of a union's intention to terminate a labor contract. Government urges unions and management alike to take full advantage of the national and state mediation and conciliation services. The principal agencies of these services are the *National Mediation Board,* the *Railroad Retirement Board,* and the *Federal Mediation and Conciliation Service.*

PRIVATE LABOR-RELATIONS WORK

In addition to union, management, and government labor-relations work there is a comparative "newcomer" to the field whose importance shows every evidence of increasing as the years go by. We refer to the rapidly growing group of workers who have never served in private industry, nor in any union, nor in government. Instead they serve in a *private capacity*—and most effectively. As a new source of endeavor, they are attracting some of the best talent in the country in the cause of better labor-management relations.

Among many others, there are three capacities in which private effort in the field can be made: (1) *labor law;* (2) *educational services;* and (3) *arbitration.*

1. *Labor Law.* A few years ago the owner of a plant and the business agent of a union could conduct all the negotiations and settle all the differences concerned with both sides of the labor-management picture. Now, even in smaller companies, the labor lawyer has become a familiar figure in almost all dealings between management and unions. His position is a crucial one, for he can contribute to labor peace or he can sow distrust and strife, even wholesale class warfare.

The labor lawyer can work for management or labor. He can remain in private practice or he can seek work with a law firm which specializes in labor work. His course of action is strictly a matter of choice. His basic requirement is a thorough-going knowledge of labor law and human nature.

2. *The Arbitrator.* There often comes a point in negotiations between labor and management when, despite all earnest efforts to arrive at an agreement, a solution still is not forth-coming. At this stage an outside expert is necessary to assess the fine points of all arguments and render a fair and impartial verdict.

This outside expert is the arbitrator. He is called by different titles—*conciliator, impartial arbitrator, impartial chairman.* Sometimes there is more than one of these men, and when this happens, usually a *tripartite board* is formed. Sometimes these jobs are permanent; sometimes they are temporary. Often an independent arbitration association is called on to suggest such arbitrators.

The arbitrator acts as a referee and should approach his task with tact and diplomacy. Generally he is a professor or a lawyer, a clergyman, or any private citizen who has distinguished himself by the fairness of his attitude and his knowledge of labor law and practices.

As a rule, arbitrators are selected from professional groups, but this is not always so. Take the case of Hugh Sheridan, for example.

Hugh started as a trucker in the Greater New York area and was a member of the Longshoremen's Union. Later he entered the trucking business with a partner and became one of the most successful operators in the field. Because of his former union association, his relations with laboring men in general was excellent.

During the early 1930s the business decline brought a large number of work stoppages in the trucking industry. To meet the situation, it was decided that an arbitration authority should be set up. The unanimous choice for the position of chief arbitrator was Hugh Sheridan. Although he had no formal education, Hugh proceeded to handle the job most effectively. As one man said of him: *"He has the natural law written in his heart."*

Such a recommendation is the best one for any job in arbitration or in labor relations.

The *consultant* is similar to the arbitrator, though with this difference: he is called in *before* there is trouble or disagreement.

3. *Educational Services.* Much could be said about the numerous schools, agencies, and groups which provide special courses in labor relations, personnel, supervisory training, labor law, and so on. The field is becoming so vast, however, that we can do no more than mention the fact of their existence briefly and then emphasize this one point: the best way for teachers in these schools to insure that their full potential for good is used is to urge more people with high purpose and sound ideas to enter the vital field of labor.

PREPARING FOR A CAREER IN LABOR RELATIONS

It has been aptly said that jobs in labor relations of any kind are not for "Johnny-Come-Latelys." One does not begin in labor relations. Time must be spent in a union, in a business organization, or in school, to acquire the proper training and experience. Some jobs demand specialized training, others do not; but all require that one must be prepared to begin at the bottom.

Thus it is imperative that the one interested in seeking a career in this vital field set his sights on his long-term objective and then begin to prepare himself for reaching his goal.

Labor relations are human relations, and human relations are moral relations. That is what makes this field a challenging one but also a great prize to whoever controls it. It is understood that he should be firmly grounded in spiritual principles. The good labor-relations man must have a genuine love of people, must be a good student of labor problems, a good psychologist, and a good moralist. By some study, observation, and sympathetic experience in dealing with people in the labor field, one can become proficient in this work.

One who aims at advancing in it should try to familiarize himself as much as possible with such subjects as *economics, labor law, public speaking, parliamentary procedure,* and *getting along with people,* especially by *knowing their problems.* These subjects offer a solid platform for the aspirant to success in any of the labor-relations jobs or professions.

PRIMACY OF THE SPIRIT

But success in the field is not enough. The great need is for spiritually inspired individuals whose aim is not so much success as it is the propagation of those basic God-given truths which have been so roundly ignored in all the major fields of influence. Therefore, *more basic than technical equipment are moral integrity and correct ideals.*

Toward this a grounding in such moral principles as *honesty* and *justice,* particularly as applied to labor problems, is a must for a Christopher-minded worker in labor relations. It is not the intention of the Christophers to teach these principles and their applications. The reader is referred to the many excellent texts, courses, and other sources of learning in Christian moral and social tenets.

The fundamentally spiritual stand of the Christophers is simple, and it is acceptable to all who desire to re-establish the original foundations of American civilization and apply them to the field of labor relations. It is as follows:

God is the Father of the whole human family, in which all are brothers in Christ, and so all human relations should be ruled by justice and charity.

Each individual is endowed with a divinely given worth and dignity which entitle him to the right to live decently and which forbid that he be used as a commodity or an inferior.

Co-operation in place of antagonism or strife is the guiding rule of all relations in economic and social matters. Labor management is a team with the common goal of labor peace and increased prosperity.

WHILE THERE IS YET TIME

The challenge is there, and the strong will take it. Labor relations, this new and growing field, is rich in job opportunities for those with high purpose. Standards are high and competition is increasing in the field. Nowhere else is there a stronger incentive for the person who will be a Christ-bearer to accept the challenge and win this trophy for Christ and for America.

FOR ADDITIONAL READING

GOLDEN, CLINTON S., and HAROLD J. RUTTENBERG. *The Dynamics of Industrial Democracy.* New York: Harper & Bros., 1942. Pp. xxvi + 358.

JOHNSON, ROBERT WOOD. *Or Forfeit Freedom.* Garden City, New York: Doubleday and Co., 1947. Pp. xi + 271.

KRIEDT, PHILIP H. and MARGARET BENTSON. *Jobs in Industrial Relations.* Minneapolis: Industrial Relations Center, University of Minnesota, January 1947; Bulletin Number 3; prepared under the direction of Dale Yoder and others. P. 57.

MILLER, RAYMOND J. *Forty Years After.* St. Paul: Radio Replies Press, 1948. P. 328.

PETERSON, FLORENCE. *Careers in Labor Relations.* Chicago: Science Research Association, 228 South Wabash, 1947; American Job Series. P. 48.

SMYTHE, D. M. *Careers in Personnel Work.* New York: E. P. Dutton & Co., 1946. P. 253.

TREACY, REV. GERALD C., S.J. *Five Great Encyclicals.* New York: The Paulist Press, 1939; with discussion club outlines. P. 215.

Your Department of Labor, Its Organization and Services, U. S. Department of Labor, Washington 25, D.C.

SPIRITUALIZING SOCIAL SERVICE

1.

A Privilege and a Responsibility

The popular concept of social service is that of some public-spirited citizen taking it upon himself to bring a basket of food or a bundle of clothing to some family in need.

Such a concept might have been more or less adequate in years long past. Today, however, the field of social service is so vast and complex that in a wide variety of ways—from child welfare to medical and psychiatric social work, and from community social planning to the specialized field of social research—its activities touch the lives of millions the country over. At present, social-service agencies and institutions require more than *one hundred thousand skilled social workers* to carry on their various programs. In 1947 the Family Service Association of America reported that, through its member agencies alone, case work services were made available to more than fifty-five million people, or approximately 40 per cent of the population of the United States!

The field of social work, then, is a tremendous one and growing with every passing year. However, while the need for social services has increased, it is encouraging to know that the caliber of the personnel in the field has kept step with the demands on their time and energies.

By and large, those who staff the various social-work agencies and administer their facilities are men and women of high purpose and a deep sense of dedication. A case in point is a twenty-eight-year-old ex-Army Air Force captain from Oklahoma. After four years in the South Pacific during the war, he returned home with the firmly fixed desire to do something in a positive way to relieve the sufferings of humanity. He turned to social service because he believed, as he put it, that "Christian principles are sorely needed in social work . . . and I'm going to try to help put them there."

NOTHING STOPPED HIM

He had no previous experience, but he didn't let that stand in his way. He headed straight for his local Welfare Department and sold them on the idea that they needed him. At the end of a year's time he had more than proved his worth. In fact, his work with teen-age boys was so outstanding that the Welfare Agency obtained a scholarship for him to attend one of the country's leading social-service schools and gave him a year's leave of absence with pay! "He is one of the best things that's happened around here," the agency supervisor explained, in commenting on the move. "We're looking for more young people with the same qualities as he has."

ANOTHER EXAMPLE

A girl from the midwest, with a wonderful record of service and influence for good in the social-work field, is another example of high-minded purpose and dedication that comes to mind.

When she graduated from college she was undecided as to what she should do in life, what career she should follow. Then one day a woman neighbor suggested that as long as she wasn't doing anything at the moment she might like to volunteer for a few hours' work each day down at her office.

"I didn't even know what her office was," this girl confessed. "But I was glad to be occupied for a few hours, so I agreed. It wasn't long before I learned that my neighbor headed our local social-welfare department. In the beginning I worked two or three hours a day on a volunteer basis, reading records, filing, recording. By the end of the third day I was working *eight* hours and was glad to be made a full-fledged member of the staff. The more I worked, the more I realized how much more I should know . . . so I started going to night school. After I graduated, I went on to get my master's degree in Social Service. All of this took a lot of effort, but it was worth it. It was time well spent."

Today this tireless worker is a Student Unit Supervisor in Social Service at one of our leading universities. We saw her just after she received the appointment, and we won't soon forget her remarks.

"I can hardly wait to get into this job," she said. "I'm getting a bit along in years, and I want to make sure that the young blood coming into social work benefits from what I have learned. There is so much need to give . . . and I feel by giving the little I have to a lot of others, God will increase it a thousandfold."

BY WAY OF EXPLANATION

Social work is a skilled method of working with individuals to help them solve problems that arise in their lives. The problem may be the loss of a job, coupled with illness in the family. It may be differences within a family which threaten an eventual breakup, with the resultant scattering of whatever children may be a part of the family unit. Or it may be conditions arising out of a home environment which necessitate social-service assistance along medical or psychiatric lines.

Years ago, when ours was a much less complex society, it was possible for neighbors, friends, and relatives to help out a family or individual in distress until the situation had righted itself. If the head of the family lost his job, the town tradesmen usually extended credit, and frequently the more fortunate members of the community helped out as well. If ill-health struck and finances were low, the doctor's bills could be spread out over a fairly lengthy period of time. Then, again, in this relatively uncomplicated existence, the opportunities for children to lead happy, wholesome lives were greater. There was a real communal spirit which carried over into almost everything that anyone did.

But society, of course, has changed, and with it have changed the needs of its citizens. Because of this there have been enacted unemployment insurance, social-security, health, and other legislative benefits covering the majority of our people.

Today the facilities of social service can be used wherever problems arise in human relationships, and the assistance of social workers is sought in a variety of ways in connection with the programs listed above. For example, social-insurance administrators are using social workers to help determine benefits due those covered under social-security laws. Likewise, state and federal authorities, charged with the administration of child-welfare programs and the measures taken to combat juvenile delinquency, call upon social-service workers for aid and advice.

Assistance of this sort is, of course, highly commendable. Nevertheless, it is important that the extension of social service avoid a common dangerous tendency of our day: namely, to weaken the self-reliance of the individual and the family by encouraging them to depend too much on public or private welfare agencies. The worker who is dominated by true love of God and country will see to it that as much responsibility as possible remains with the individual and the family.

Those who are hostile to God and country see in social service an excellent means to do just the opposite—to make each and all so dependent on government that eventually the state will dominate their bodies *and* their souls.

PRIVATE AGENCIES

Not all social work, of course, is performed under governmental administration or direction. Far from it. And this is desirable for the very good reason that, wherever and whenever possible, local communities should work toward solving their own social problems.

As regards *private* social-service agencies and institutions, the Family Service Association of America comprises some two hundred and fifty divisions. In addition there is a large number of non-Catholic (90) and Catholic (160) agencies which administer primarily to their own groups. Also there are other independent sectarian and non-sectarian agencies apart from any of these groups.

TREMENDOUS OPPORTUNITY

In the realm of social service there is an extraordinary opportunity to recapture and restore the divine inspiration which is the very foundation of social work. Those who take up full-time careers in this vital field should lead the way as champions of the one great essential in work of this kind: that God in heaven is solicitous about even the least of His children.

A powerful reminder of this earnest concern of God for man's welfare in this life is contained in the unusual answer Christ gave to the messengers of John the Baptist who were sent to find out whether or not he was the true Messiah. *"Go and relate to John what you have heard and seen,"* Christ declared, almost abruptly. *"The blind see, the lame walk, the lepers are cleansed, the deaf hear, the dead rise again, the poor have the gospel preached to them."* (Matthew 11:4,5)

Only the last point of the six mentioned in Christ's statement dealt with the strictly spiritual. But even in that there was a reproach to those who should know better than to neglect to pass on to the poor of the world the Truth intended for *all* men.

The other five points Christ mentioned concern the *physical* sufferings of mankind. Here indeed is a strange yet wonderful proof He gave of His Divinity! He could have given a hundred other testimonies instead of choosing this one. He didn't refer to Himself directly. He spoke only of the effects on others of the flow of God's love in heaven through Him to afflicted man on earth.

YOUR SOCIAL SERVICE TOO

Since God in heaven is solicitous for afflicted man on earth, He expects each and every one of us to show a sincere love for the unfortunate, a love that is more than wishful thinking, a love that expresses itself in a much more positive way than merely giving a dime to a hungry man and telling him to buy a sandwich.

God expects every one of us to play some role, no matter how small, in a personal, individual manner. This approach is the indispensable foundation for organized social work. God means that, in a very literal way, each of us should feed the hungry, give drink to the thirsty, harbor the homeless, visit the sick.

These are tasks in which everyone can participate. There is not one person who cannot perform, once a day, once a week, once a month, or even once a year, a corporal work of mercy—an act of love to Christ through one of His poor, without any thought of recompense, with no strings attached.

If you can't think of a case which needs your help, it shouldn't take more than two minutes to find one out . . . from your church, your doctor, the police department, or from one of many social-service agencies which are in great need of volunteer help to assist the trained workers and thus release them for cases that require more intensive treatment. We believe that millions of men and women throughout the country can be found to make their less fortunate neighbors their personal concern. And once they do, by their sheer weight of numbers and by the grace of God working through them, they could, overnight, do much to deepen that spiritual motivation which is so essential to the social-service field.

In addition such individual participation would have other advantages: (1) It might stir thousands more to take up full-time careers in social service; (2) countless others in all walks of life would, by their very interest, have a leavening influence on the whole field of social-service work. In a hundred different ways they could prevent it from becoming despiritualized and regimented. They would stop other abuses which inevitably creep in when the individual becomes just another cold, impersonal case.

First, last, and always, the responsibility remains with the individual. The organized social-service field is simply the outgrowth of individual participation. The function of the organized field is to supplement those services which the individual is unable to supply. The trained worker in social service is the representative of the individual citizen. He or she has been delegated a responsibility to service those areas of need where the individual citizen is not competent to render adequate assistance. But it should not be forgotten for one moment that this responsibility is *only delegated*. The individual citizen still has a personal obligation—and one of the best ways to keep alive that sense of individual responsibility is to follow the formula of Christ and do a bit of it yourself—"feed the hungry . . . harbor the homeless . . . visit the sick . . ."

A PUBLIC DUTY

In general, social work is carried on by departments of welfare and assistance, health groups and hospitals, bureaus of social insurance, public recreation centers, juvenile courts and correction agencies, child-guidance and adult clinics, neighborhood settlement houses, family-welfare and child-welfare societies, community chests and councils, institutions for the handicapped, and many others.

Obviously, those who maintain and operate these facilities play an influential role in the increasing and continuous long-term planning for community and national life.

They help to meet *four general problems:* (1) economic need, (2) health, (3) behavior, and (4) the use of leisure time. Moreover, they help to meet these problems *through the use of scientific knowledge and methods.*

In subsequent discussions the social-service field will be analyzed in detail with reference to the opportunities available to those who would enter this sphere with a Christlike purpose.

For the moment, however, we should like to re-emphasize the point that was touched on earlier in this chapter: namely, that all social work should be rooted in the divine. Those we wish to encourage to take up full-time careers in this important field should be ever aware of the *sacred worth of every human being, made as he is in the image and likeness of God.* In helping to ensure more lasting blessings to many here, and over the world, who are finding the battle of life ever more difficult, they will be spurred on by the knowledge that, as Christ Himself put it: *"As long as you did it to one of these my least brethren, you did it to me."* (Matthew 25:40)

Without that emphasis, without that clear-cut concept, the best of social programs runs the risk of failing to fulfill its fundamental purpose. It likewise can become a potent weapon in the hands of those who would undermine our country and everything for which it stands. When roots are planted only in the material, without any spiritual motivation, the end result is that man is considered merely as an animal and treated as such. As T. S. Eliot put it so clearly: *"The last temptation is the greatest treason: to do the right deed for the wrong reason."*

With the proper motivation, however, the words Pope Pius XI spoke on the urgent necessity of rebuilding the social order will come closer to realization.

"It will be possible," he said, *"to unite all men in harmonious striving for the common good only when all sections of human society have the intimate conviction that they are members of a single human family and children of the same heavenly Father; and further that they are one body in Christ and everyone members one of another."*

2.

Divisions of the Field

"One of the most exhilarating feelings in the world is knowing that you have helped others in times of need . . . have helped them benefit by what you have enjoyed."

These words of a twenty-four-year-old social worker from Syracuse well express the attitude of most of those in this vital sphere. Such an attitude likewise explains why thousands of men and women make social service their *lifetime* careers in spite of the sacrifices that are sometimes involved or the depressing social conditions with which they constantly come face to face.

Few people who are true social workers choose to leave the field. They find in their work a satisfaction and an understanding of the problems of others which few occupations afford. Each day brings new opportunities to help people live better, and undoubtedly this accounts for the fact that *3 per cent of all professional people work in social service.*

The measure of love—love of one's fellow man for love of God—is *service*. It is within the province of social workers to be instrumental in bringing to suffering humanity a measure of that compassion and love of Christ which surpass all understanding.

The way each social worker "changes the world" will depend upon the strength of his or her purpose and the extent of his or her perseverance. *Truth* will have its effect not only by the mere presentation of it but perhaps even more by *actual performance,* by reducing theory to practice.

IDEAS HAVE POWER

Since social work deals with people and their problems so directly, the influence of a worker in this field cannot be overestimated. His ideas on a wide variety of subjects will inevitably pass over into the minds of his clients, just as what is in a teacher's mind is transmitted to the students in the classroom.

When the social worker's ideas are rooted in God-given principles, tremendous good can be effected.

On the other hand, when—as occasionally happens—the social worker's ideas are warped or colored with a godless philosophy, the client receives distorted impressions: that man is but a creature of passion, has no free will, is dominated by unconscious impulses of a lustful nature, and so on. From this pagan concept it is but a step to the acceptance of the notion that man is but an economic animal and that whatever rights he has come from the state. This acceptance is hastened when it is remembered that people with whom the social worker has to deal are often emotionally unsettled because they are improperly housed, inadequately fed or clothed, without sufficient medical care and advice, lacking any real economic security.

A person entering this field with a Christlike purpose, convinced of his own essential dignity and of the intrinsic worth of those whom his profession serves, has the ready-made opportunity to practice the virtue of charity daily, even hourly, and so fulfill the command of Christ to "love thy neighbor." A social worker has the vocation of helping to put individuals back on their feet and giving them the chance of more easily working out their eternal destiny.

Incidentally, it might be well to repeat here the words which are used in the section devoted to federal government regarding the delegation of responsibility. In the field of social service, nothing should be done by the federal government that more properly should be done by state government. Nor should the state assume responsibilities that belong to the city or town. By the same token, the individual citizen should not allow the city, state, or federal government to do in the realm of social service what he, the individual citizen, can and should do for his less fortunate fellow men.

Generally speaking, social-service agencies are divided into governmental services (federal, state, and local), paid for by taxes, and private or voluntary services, supported by contributions, bequests, or part-payment fees.

Social work is further broken down into *social case work, social group work,* and *community organization work.* Social case work is itself divided into (1) family case work, (2) child-welfare assistance, (3) medical social aid, and (4) psychiatric social work. To all the above can be added the two divisions of social *research* and social *administration.*

SOCIAL CASE WORK

Strictly defined, social case work is a technique of working with human beings on a *person-to-person basis,* rather than with people in large numbers. A social case worker must know and understand the scientific principles which underlie individual behavior and must be able to apply these principles in his chosen career. But above and beyond this knowledge he must have a profound interest in people as individuals. An interest, for example, similar to that of a young lady from Maryland who wanted, as she put it, "to be so much a vital part of the world I'm living in, and to help others to be a part of it," that she began, even as a freshman in college, to think of a social-service career.

"Our college was just becoming interested in social service at the time," she told us, "and one of the first things they did was to arrange field trips to stimulate our interest. It took me only a few such trips to realize that this was the field for me. My family, however, had other plans for me and didn't take kindly to the idea. They sent me abroad for a year to 'get over the notion.'

"It was a miserable twelve months, I can tell you," she went on. "I was constantly plagued with the realization that I was idling away time that could be spent in helping others who were in such dire need. But perhaps it was a good thing in a way, too, for ever since I have been working twice as hard to make up for that year I wasted. I only hope I succeed."

FAMILY CASE WORK

Family case work deals with the greatest variety of human situations. The social worker counsels and helps people troubled by economic distress, illness, personality maladjustments, family friction, broken homes, or poor management of those homes. The ideal here is to build up and strengthen the bonds of family life within the framework of true Christian living.

Sometimes the problems are fairly simple and the solutions easily arrived at. But more often than not the problems are quite complex, requiring skill and tact. The social worker may help a person understand and modify feelings that stand in the way of making a marriage a success. He may arrange for some financial assistance to tide a family over a difficult period. Or he may recommend treatment by a psychiatrist to straighten out a mental or emotional condition. The social worker in each and every situation has to see the person and problem *objectively*, has to get to the root of the trouble while still seeing to it that human dignity is not sacrificed thereby.

CHILD WELFARE

This division of social work is concerned with the care, protection, and placement of dependent children who are neglected, delinquent, physically handicapped, or mentally defective, and whose welfare is endangered by unwholesome conditions in the home, community, or place of employment. Many children live in families that lack economic security, healthful environment, and affection—things which every child needs. In situations like these the social worker maintains close contact with other social workers who are on the staffs of child-guidance clinics, schools, and juvenile courts. He tries to do everything in his power to resolve difficulties without resort to drastic remedies which may prove a tremendous shock to the mental and emotional balance of the parties concerned.

Probation officers are social workers, though the average person does not think of them as such. These officers are attached to the juvenile courts and deal with children who have violated the law. When a child comes before the court, for example, the duty of these social workers is to investigate the youngster's background, his or her home, environment, school, friends—the object being to find out how the child got to the point where he or she knowingly violated the law.

One such social worker in the South—a volunteer—put her Christopher purpose to good use when she became concerned at the treatment of wayward girl minors in her community. To familiarize herself with the various cases, she appointed herself a "committee of one" and attended hearings in court. There she learned to her amazement that there was no suitable place provided to which these delinquents could be sent for discipline and proper training. On her own initiative, she formed a group whose function was to raise money and secure permission to establish a young women's resident home where girls in need of special attention could be directed.

The job wasn't easy, but the welfare worker's perseverance and Christlike motive "paid off." A home was eventually established to which neglected youngsters, as well as those actively delinquent, could be sent. Since its founding, hundreds of girls have been rehabilitated and made responsible members of the community.

MEDICAL SOCIAL WORK

This division is concerned with handicapped individuals who are under a physician's care, in clinic, hospital, or medical-service programs. It is carried forward on a teamwork basis, with the physician and others involved co-operating in setting the patient to rights again.

Many medical social workers go in for public medical-health programs of federal, state, and local governments for crippled children, the blind, et cetera. And here, it should be stressed, there is an increasing number of projects in research open to workers in this particular field. What better way is there, too, for a Christopher to carry out Christ's command when He said: *"They that are in health need not a physician, but they*

*that are ill. Go then and learn what this meaneth: I will have
mercy and not sacrifice. For I am not come to call the just,
but sinners."* (Matthew 9:12–13)

PSYCHIATRIC SOCIAL WORK

While medical social service deals primarily with problems
of physical illness, psychiatric social work is concerned with
mental illness and defects and the more serious emotional difficulties. Psychiatric social workers are employed in child-
guidance clinics, mental hospitals, military institutions, as well
as in general social-work fields. The psychiatric social worker
is equipped to deal with and help mentally disturbed people
who are under a doctor's care. However, there are limits to the
worker's concern: he merely takes care of the *social* aspects of
the case. The psychiatrist sees to the *professional treatment*.

COMMUNITY ORGANIZATION

Social work which has to do with the organization, planning,
and co-ordinating of community programs, and the budgeting
and public-relations work regarding these same programs, is
called *community organization work*. Co-ordinating councils of
social-service agencies are set up to represent the various
private and public agencies that operate on a community level
and thus avoid any tendency to overlap on the services rendered. Often these councils are consulted by the membership
agencies in matters of formulating agency policy, functions,
programming, and publicity.

GROUP WORK

The youngest of the social-service divisions is *group work*,
yet it has already assumed stature in the field. Group workers
are most effective in settlement houses, boy- and girl-scout programs, in group therapy among patients in mental hospitals, in
rehabilitation of juvenile delinquents, and other similar projects. Each individual in the group contributes to the group
according to his capicity. At the same time the group, under

the guiding influence of the group worker, helps the individual as much as it can.

SOCIAL RESEARCH

The primary function of research personnel is to bring facts together for purposes of social planning. These workers make special surveys or engage in research projects for the analysis of community needs or the evaluation of an agency program. Sometimes these projects extend to a national level, and for the person who combines interest in scientific methods with the desire to keep in touch with vital human problems, social research is stimulating work. Social *legislation,* housing, slum clearance, and other similar measures result from such research.

SOCIAL ADMINISTRATION

The more highly qualified and capable social workers are usually promoted to administrative duties. *And here, as elsewhere in the social-service field, it is important that the worker with a Christopher purpose should set the pace—should lead the way in the direction which he wishes others to follow.*

Administrative work involves supervising and directing case workers, planning budgets, in-service training, public-relations projects, and carrying on other administrative activities—all geared to develop programs, help groups, advance community initiative, and expand resources to the end that a healthier, more satisfying, and fuller way of life—under God—may be achieved.

THE TRUE CONCEPT

Since the true concept of social service for all men, regardless of race, color, or creed, owes its origin to Christ, it will be the privilege of those who enter this vital field to keep that concept ever alive. Without it, there is little chance that the beneficial effects of social service will continue for very long, for it will be very much like trying to keep a house warm after the fire in the furnace has died out. The house may feel warm for a time. But this is because of the leftover heat that was generated while the fire was still burning. When that lingering warmth vanishes and the furnace is cold, then suffering is bound to follow until the source of the heat is rekindled once more.

So long as social-service work keeps its roots firmly planted in the divine, so long will it continue to achieve its objective—an objective in keeping with Him Who had "compassion on the multitude."

3.

Qualifications and Opportunities

Some years ago in Milwaukee a young man was stricken with a near-fatal illness which kept him in a hospital bed for almost eighteen months. Lying there day after weary day, he soon tired of thinking about his own misfortune and began to think of the suffering in the world outside. He promised God that if he ever got well enough again, he would spend the rest of his life helping others in distress.

Eventually he did recover and set out to keep his promise. When he went to college he took a "pre-med" course, in the hope that one day he would become a doctor. When someone suggested a career in social service instead, the idea appalled him. The thought of living with other people's troubles—which in his mind was the beginning and end of social work—disturbed him even while it repelled him. He decided to find out more about it. And the more he learned, the more he wanted to learn.

Today this man has an important research job in social service. His contributions to the field have been recognized publicly a number of times. But his greatest satisfaction comes from fulfilling the plan he laid out for himself when he was invalided in the hospital years before. "I feel now as I did then," he will tell you. "If I help just one person a day, by the time I'm an old man I'll have helped thousands. It's the least I can do for all that God has done for me."

As we have said, social work is a *profession*. It follows, therefore, that the best way to enter the field is to prepare oneself adequately for it. A primary requisite in this direction is to earn a degree from an accredited school of social work. This is most important. Despite the shortage of social workers, reputable social-service agencies are reluctant to employ those who are not professionally trained.

Social workers with graduate training will find excellent employment opportunities. Those without it, however, will have to face increasingly difficult competition. Yet, despite this, the federal government does offer employment openings to workers who lack a social-service-school degree. Qualification for these openings can be met by certain types of social-work *experience* or by a combination of *training and experience*. Specifically, the requirements are as follows:

> One year of training in an accredited school of social work, including field work and courses in psychiatric and medical information. In addition the following experience is needed for the different grades in the social-service field:
>
> 1. *Social Worker* (average)
> One year's experience in *social case work* in a health or welfare agency.
> 2. *Chief Social Worker* (subregional office)
> Three years' experience, including at least two years in psychiatric or medical social work, or one full year of supervisory work.
> 3. *Case Supervisor*
> Three years' experience, but the supervisory work does *not* have to be in the psychiatric or medical field.
> 4. *Chief and Assistant Chief Social Worker* (hospital or regional office)

Four years' experience, including two years of supervisory work in psychiatric or medical social work and two years of administrative experience in social case work.

5. *Assistant Chief, Social Service Station* (branch office)

A master's degree or graduation from an accredited school of social work, and three years of administrative experience in social work, including a year in a responsible administrative capacity.

6. *Chief, Social Service Section* (hospital, regional, branch, or central office)

A master's degree or graduation from an accredited school of social work, plus experience indicating ability to administer a large-scale program.

No written test is given for social-work civil-service positions. Applicants are judged and appointed on the basis of the training and experience indicated on their completed applications.

A WORD ABOUT SOCIAL SERVICE SCHOOLS

In the United States today there are approximately fifty-three graduate social-work schools accredited by the American Association of Schools of Social Work.

From the professional and scientific viewpoint the courses offered in these schools are excellent. However, it should be pointed out that the learning of techniques and theory of social work should not comprise the whole of social-service indoctrination. It isn't enough to grasp the fundamentals of sociology, psychology, biology, economics, and so on. A person must be schooled in learning about the *complete* man—and the eternal destiny for which God created him.

Wherever and whenever this emphasis is not imparted, we suggest—in fact, urge—that the social worker find the means to supplement his formal training with the view to supplying what may be lacking in his formal education.

ENTRANCE REQUIREMENTS

Entrance requirements of these schools are all about the same: namely, a bachelor's degree, including undergraduate courses in social and biological sciences, and a satisfactory level of scholastic achievement.

Note: Studies have shown that men enter social work with somewhat less academic education and much less professional training than do women. Enrollment of men in schools of social work, however, has increased appreciably in recent years. In 1940, for example, nearly one fourth of those who attended social-service schools, and about the same proportion of those who received degrees or certificates upon completion of training, were men.

Incidentally, various private agencies are currently offering scholarships to applicants who possess the proper qualifications. Detailed information may be obtained by writing to such agencies, which have shown a commendable desire to cooperate with the public in alleviating shortages of trained personnel in the social-service field.

PART-TIME POSITIONS

The Veterans Administration has established a number of part-time, paid, field-work positions. Students who have been accepted for the second-year curriculum in an accredited school of social work and have had a year of experience in a health or welfare agency are eligible to apply. Salaries for these training positions are prorated on an hourly basis, and a minimum of twenty-four hours of work a week is required.

Applications for these positions should be forwarded to the Director, Personnel Service, of the VA branch office which covers the area in which the applicant resides or desires to reside upon completion of training. *Application should be submitted on the US Standard Form 57 and marked as request for "Social Work Field Position."*

Also—and this is apart from Veterans Administration positions—an organization in New York called the Social Work

Vocational Service maintains a listing of upward of three hundred jobs for social workers all over the country and outside the New York area. New York listings are left to local agencies.

NOT JUST A PROFESSION

While the salaries in the social-service field compare favorably with those in other professions—and the current trend is *upward*—nevertheless this should *not* be the motivation which impels a person to take up social work as a lifetime career.

Social service is a *vocation* as well as a profession, and sometimes a degree of sacrifice may be required of the prospective social worker. A letter we received about a year ago from a young man in New Orleans tells far better than any words of ours the spirit in which a true Christ-bearer should enter this vital field.

Several years ago [he wrote] I gave up a $10,000 advertising job to take up the religious life. It wasn't very long, however, before I realized that such a life was not for me, and so I came out into the world again. Unfortunately, I made the same mistake of taking a job just for the big money involved—$7,000 this year, maybe $9,000 or $10,000 next year. But always in the back of my mind was the feeling that social work was my forte. . . .

Well, to make a long story short, I am resigning my job to begin as a Welfare Visitor at $175 a month. Back in college I had a year or so of training in social work and so the shift won't be too difficult. I especially like to work with young people and I intend, if possible, to get into that branch of social service as soon as I can. Since I've made the change, incidentally, I've become increasingly aware of the truth of one particular line you put in your *Christopher News Notes*. "The world is divided into two classes of people," you said. "Those who do things, and those who take the credit." I intend to belong to the first class. I'm sure there'll be far less competition!

219

PERSONALITY REQUIREMENTS

All that has been written so far has not taken into consideration the personality requirements of the prospective social-service worker.

The effective social worker must have a good mind and be blessed with common sense. With these qualities should be combined a faculty for remaining pleasant under all circumstances and a consciousness of responsibility. A sincere interest in people and an abiding faith in their fundamental goodness are indispensable. Dealing with those who are not behaving normally requires patience, adaptability, resourcefulness, and sound judgment. It means, too, that the social worker *himself* must be mentally and emotionally well balanced, in good health, and possess a real joy in living.

This matter of being mentally and emotionally well balanced is particularly important in the specialized fields of social service most in need of trained, sound-thinking men and women: fields such as *Parole, Probation, Board of Education Attendance Departments, Child Guidance, Group Work, Psychiatric Social Work, Penology and Prison Administration,* and *Criminology.*

THE CHRISTOPHER PURPOSE

To be a Christ-bearer is to *do* something. And to *do* is to *go* into the dust and heat of the market place bearing Christ and His love and compassion to those unfortunates of the world who need them so badly.

The aim of the social worker's effort might be compared to that of the Christians in France following the end of World War II, as related by Claire Huchet Bishop in her book, *France Alive.* Pointing out that the goal is not the "salvation of each individual alone," Miss Bishop goes on to say:

> *. . . The final sign, the one Christ gave us, is charity toward neighbor through love of God: By that sign you will be known as My disciples, if you love one another . . . Supernatural life is not an outer garment . . . super-*

natural life should transform natural life; the love of God should blossom into love of neighbor. Then, and then only, has the pagan evolved into a Christian. All Christianity is incarnated in life.

The social worker who is fired by the Christopher purpose, who is concerned with man's welfare here as well as hereafter, can help bring to suffering humanity the world over a little of that peace and comfort which the Creator of *all* meant to be the lot of *all* mankind.

4.

Hard Work—and Fundamentals

The old saying that to be forewarned is to be forearmed applies as much to the field of social service as to any of the other vital spheres. As one recognized authority in social work observed not long ago: "Those who crave a magician's power cannot succeed as social workers. It takes someone who is tough enough to face life as it is and yet who has the faith that life is worth living in spite of the pain that must sometime be endured. Such a person will not find it 'depressing' to work with people in trouble. . . ."

Countless examples are brought to the attention of Christopher headquarters each year, showing the Christlike motives which spark men and women in all parts of the country to take up lifetime careers as social workers. There are many we should like to retell were sufficient space available. However, one particularly inspiring case of a woman who is now a training consultant for the Federal Bureau of Public Assistance does bear repeating now.

Years ago she was a young kindergarten teacher assigned to a public school on the poor side of town. It was her first experience with poverty, and she soon discovered that some of her children were failing to learn, not because of a lack of intelligence, but because they were undernourished. She called in a doctor, and he verified her suspicions. He told her that her pupils were using all of their energies to dress themselves and travel to school.

Curious to know if this condition prevailed elsewhere, she visited a school in a better section of the city. There she found the children well fed and cared for, with correspondingly high grades. They had all the advantages—extra books and toys, hot lunches, et cetera—denied to the youngsters under her care. "It was a great shock to my young enthusiasm," she told us, "to find two tax-supported institutions so dissimilar. I believed in humanity, believed that those who were able had a responsibility to help those less fortunate. Even then I was aware that prevention was very important. Unless the intellectual, emotional, physical, and social needs of these children were supplied, they would create personal and community problems in the future. I became more and more concerned."

At that time, she continued, she had never considered social work as a career. But the school situation changed all her previous ideas. She went back to college for two years and obtained a master's degree in social work. Then she became a social-service case worker. However, she never lost interest in teaching, as her subsequent actions testify. The public-welfare field was progressing about this time, so she aimed at and secured a post as a district field supervisor, charged with on-the-job training of young social workers. As the years went by she advanced to more responsible positions—supervisory, teaching, and administrative, by turns. Only recently she completed a year and a half's study of the social-service field for the last fifty years, a study which will prove an invaluable aid to others coming into this vital sphere. "Teaching social service is especially gratifying," she told us. "And I honestly think our country is going to be 'hard put' if we don't get more and better social-work instructors."

SOMETHING TO GUARD AGAINST

Most of the social-service schools in America furnish excellent technical and professional training, as we mentioned earlier. However, it is a fact that there are some godless-minded professors teaching sociology, economics, government, psychology, and other social studies. These professors doubt or deny the existence of a Supreme Being, the essential worth of the individual human soul, and the freedom of the will. And much of the teaching of these men logically leads to the acceptance of the totalitarian state even though they themselves may not carry their theorizing to its final conclusion.

For many of them the only source of human rights is society itself. What society gives, they reason, society can take away. To paraphrase the words of one of the founders of American sociology, custom is king and custom finds its way into law. If, for example, society adopted the custom of putting aged people to death, then—in the opinion of these men —this custom would be perfectly acceptable. All right and wrong, in their view, are relative to the society in which people live.

MUST RETURN TO MORAL LAW

The danger to our Christian civilization inherent in such a philosophy is becoming more and more apparent to sound-thinking Americans all over the country. As one distinguished professional man, Dr. F. L. Feierabend, writing in the *Journal of the American Medical Association,* pointed out:

> *Physicians must reject the teaching of the materialist sociologists and return to the teachings of the moral law. They must reject completely the doctrine of the materialist, which teaches that religion, and morality, is the opium of the people and that man is motivated entirely by instinct. Doctors must avoid this materialistic doctrine or by their acts they will be promoting regimentation. Neglect of social responsibility invites the State to take over with coercion and regimentation.*

Social workers in public agencies are often assigned to handle cases in which the doctor has advised therapeutic abortion, sterilization, or artificial birth control. Highly complex cases, requiring sound moral judgment, the proper placing of children, and so on, also come within the scope of social-service work.

Finally, social workers from time to time come in contact with cases that require the attention of skilled psychiatric diagnosis and treatment. When, as occasionally happens, such diagnosis and treatment run counter to the moral law, it is the duty of the social worker to call that fact to the attention of his or her superiors and take whatever steps are necessary to correct the condition. In a large midwestern hospital not so long ago just such a situation occurred.

A young girl with a moral problem had been sent by the local social-welfare department to a psychiatrist who regularly assisted in such matters. The girl was so stricken with feelings of guilt that proper readjustment was difficult for her. The psychiatrist, instead of trying to solve the problem along moral lines, made every attempt to erase her feeling of guilt by telling her that her transgressions were not sins at all and she shouldn't bother her head with them.

This approach, logically enough, only made the girl more confused. Finally she became so overwrought that the welfare authorities considered sending her to an institution. Before this step was taken, however, a sound-thinking social worker who had been working on the case asked for and received permission to see what she could do. Her first act was to advise the girl not to return to the psychiatrist. Then she enlisted a religious-minded person to help bring a sense of the spiritual back into the girl's daily life. In a few months' time the girl was well on the road to recovery and a complete readjustment to a normal life. Today she is happily married to a fine young man in the community.

THE CAUSE OF MOST SOCIAL ILLS

The root of most of our social ills today—economic insecurity, inadequate housing, insufficient wages for the present high cost of living—is not so much material as *spiritual*: the overeager pursuit of worldly goods, the exaggerated desire for possessions, the feverish ambition for more power, the incessant striving for outward success. A sociologist who works for social reform, while neglecting this widespread disease of the soul, is only treating the symptoms; he is not getting at their causes and may even be aggravating the malady.

If people lack many things they need today, basically this is not to be charged to any "system," but to the avarice in the souls of so many others, to the fact that too many think in terms of the good of the *few*, rather than of *all*. Whatever they call themselves, such people are materialistic in their thinking. And it is this very greed for material things which lies at the root of current social ills.

There is no doubt that social reform is needed; but even more, and as an indispensable foundation, there is need for a re-emphasis on fundamental principles; for, strangely enough, the one thing some who earnestly desire to help humanity forget is *man himself*. They forget he is something more than an animal to be fed, clothed, and amused. They forget that he is a person with spiritual needs which far surpass in importance any of his material wants, important as those things are. Social service itself will fall apart, will fail of the *real* purpose it was meant to serve, unless those who are possessed of a Christopher motivation go into the field and bring there the love, the truth, and the compassion of Christ. The truly Christian concept of social service will not enter the field by itself. It has been said, and so rightly, that *"ideas need legs."* The Christopher must be the bearer of Christ into the market place.

HARD WORK

Those who decide to enter social work with a Christlike purpose should be prepared to devote two years as students in a social-service school and as field workers under expert supervision. And, as was pointed out previously, care should be taken in the selection of a school so that if God-given principles are not integrated into the course of study the student should find other means of supplying what is lacking.

Incidentally, more and more sound-thinking men and women are needed in these schools, not only as instructors but to serve in administrative capacities as well. Many vacancies on the faculties of the various social-service schools are occurring all the time. In addition, each year sees *new* schools of social work come into being to satisfy the demand for trained personnel in this vital field. To fill a teaching or administrative position a master's degree is required, and a Ph.D. is preferred. In the past there have been only five or six schools in the country giving doctorates in social service, but more schools are gearing their programs to meet the ever-increasing demand for top-level personnel. It is much easier, in fact, to get a position as a teacher of social service on a university faculty than it is to get a similar post teaching some other subject.

Salaries in jobs of this type vary according to location. In New York, Pennsylvania, and California, for example, the pay is higher than in some other parts of the country. However, the over-all average is in keeping with the training and responsibility which the positions demand.

Such instructors and administrators should, of course, come from the ranks of social workers themselves. Those who aspire to careers in social work with a Christopher purpose would do well to consider teaching and administrative posts as well as social-service field work and similar positions.

IMPOSSIBLE TO DISREGARD

The belief that Christ is come to redeem us, that He is ever present, that we were made to live with Him for all eternity, makes it impossible for us to disregard His Presence and His Plan in all we think and do.

Especially is this true of those in the social-service field.

In the unfolding of the client's story the Christopher social worker sees much more than the "slings and arrows" of the misfortune to which the client has been subjected. He sees an opportunity to bring Christ into the life of an individual whose mind and heart may be so overcome with the effects of his predicament that he has forgotten what it is to feel the compassion of Him Who knew what it was to suffer.

The Christopher social worker, then, knows that man is more than what he eats. He knows that he has an immortal soul and that his final destination is God. It is the *spiritual*—as well as the emotional, intellectual, and physical—life of the client that concerns the social worker who would truly bear Christ into every phase of his chosen career.

OTHER CHRISTS

The social worker who is fired with a Christopher purpose can do tremendously far-reaching good in changing the world for the better. This is so no matter how insignificant his or her part in the social-service field may be.

Not for a moment should a Christopher forget he has his own destiny to work out here and hereafter. Yet neither should he ever lose sight of the fact that he has a like obligation toward others. There is specific definiteness on this point in the command of Christ. While He said, *"Thou shalt love thy neighbor,"* He was very careful to give the measure of how much that love should be. *"As thyself,"* He said.

There is no contesting that.

One of Christ's own apostles, St. James, is most emphatic on this point, and his words should have especial meaning for the Christopher social worker. *"Religion clean and undefiled before God and the Father,"* St. James says, *"is this: to visit the fatherless and widows in their tribulation, and to keep one's self unspotted from this world."*

Note the emphasis he puts on solicitude for others. Even if a person with weak faith starts to share with others the Truth he possesses, starts to put into practice the corporal works of mercy in the light of Christ's love, his own strength and effectiveness is increased thereby. Literally, he is putting into daily action the meaning of the words:

"For this was I born . . . that I should give testimony to the truth." (John 18:37)

FOR ADDITIONAL READING

CORA KASIUS. *Nancy Clark, Social Worker.* A novel. Dodd, Mead & Co.

Family Case Work. Find Your Career in Family Social Work. Pamphlets. Family Welfare Association of America, 192 Lexington Avenue, New York 16, N.Y.

Just a Job or a Profession? Pamphlet. Loyola University School of Social Work, 28 North Franklin Street, Chicago, Illinois.

Professional Social Work. Folder. St. Louis University School of Social Work, St. Louis 3, Missouri.

Social Work a Modern Profession of Community Service. Pamphlet. American Association of Social Work, 1 Park Ave., New York 16, N.Y.

The Social Worker. Booklet. American Association of Schools of Social Work, 1313 East 60th St., Chicago, Illinois.

SECRETARIAL WORK
WITH A PURPOSE

1.

Opportunities Galore

A young woman we know was recently offered an important post on a national magazine after she had served an apprenticeship as secretary to the editor. In the beginning she had no desire to start so far "down the ladder," as she put it. She had a particular job in mind and wanted to get it at once. However, on the advice of a Christopher friend, she took a secretarial position with the publication with the intention of preparing herself for advancement when the chance presented itself. That her purpose and perseverance paid off is evident from the letter she sent to Christopher headquarters not long ago.

"Almost a year to the day," she wrote, "I was offered the position of production manager, and during this past summer I've been in training for the job. Since these duties don't take all my time, I'm still secretary to the executive editor, learning as much as I can before I switch over to my new position. . . . Many thanks and best wishes to you and the Christophers!"

This is just one example of hundreds we could give, showing how a Christopher purpose, once aroused, has provided the "spark" for many who were unaware of the tremendous potential they possessed as secretaries in any one of the vital fields.

Some time ago a young lady in Chicago, who had just graduated from the University of Illinois, set out to get a job which, in her words, "paid well, wasn't too hard, and gave long vacations." And she succeeded.

Upon getting what she felt was the ideal position, she wrote us telling us how "well off" she was. Our reply, after a little thought, was to remind her in a friendly way that she was not only "well off" but *far off* too. We pointed out what a pity it was that so many wonderful people like herself, who could do so much to bring the peace of Christ into the main stream of American life, were so quickly winding up in dead-end streets because they thought only of themselves, while nearly all those with crackpot ideas were aiming for spots where they could make everyone else as crazy as themselves.

A few weeks later this same girl sent us a second letter, and in it was a real sense of purpose. The Christopher approach had apparently struck home. All on her own, she had shifted to another job—this time as secretarial assistant to the dean of one of the country's largest universities. Twenty-four applications had been received ahead of hers, and the director in charge of personnel refused, at first, to accept another one. However, this girl persisted in her request that she at least be allowed to file her application, and finally her request was granted.

SHE WOULDN'T TAKE NO

What followed after that would have tested the determination of even the most courageous individual. She was made to understand that although her application was put on file, her chance of getting the job ended there. She had too little experience, too little background—facts which she admitted, although she did point out that she had successfully completed an intensive course in secretarial work at a very fine business college. She was refused permission to see the dean, but she, in turn, refused to take "no" for an answer. Every day for three weeks she appeared at the university, repeating her request, until, in sheer desperation, the dean granted her an interview.

The results were surprising indeed! So impressed was he at her enthusiasm, her motivation, her sense of *purpose*, that before she was through explaining why she thought she should get the position, he told her, almost gratefully: *"Young lady, you've got the job. I only wish we had more young people like you here at the university. We could use them!"*

Undoubtedly the dean's statement was sincere, but it is doubtful that he thought his words had any special significance as far as this young woman was concerned. Yet she did take the statement to heart. Since she has been in her job she has been instrumental in getting others with her purpose and ideals into various departments at the school. She makes some forty-odd dollars a week now, whereas in private business she made about ten dollars a week more. She works harder and has less time to herself than ever before, but she doesn't mind. Now she is really living. To her it is a source of deep satisfaction to have endless opportunities to be working in a job where she can do much to make the world a bit the better because she is in it.

A secretary employed by a large business firm found in the Christopher approach the answer to her dissatisfaction with a job which she felt had "no purpose." She sent in her application to the Civil Service Commission for a position in government work, took the required test, and subsequently was placed as a secretary in an agency of the State Department. Already she has done her bit to get workers of *good* into the spheres that count—which, she is convinced, is even more important than driving out those whose purpose is to wreck our country and everything for which it stands.

The fact that this young woman did make the change-over to one of the vital fields does not mean that good, sound-thinking workers are not needed in *all* walks of life. But it should be recognized that the battle for the world today is being waged in the arena of *ideas*—and it is there that the struggle will be lost or won.

Finally, there is the case of a prominent labor official who was recently elected to office in his union. Finding the pressure of his duties exceedingly heavy, it was necessary for him to hire a full-time secretary. The young lady whom he hired has, in the course of time, taken over much of the detail work connected with the union's activities. In a certain sense she *is* this official, since the decisions she makes are backed by his authority. The wonderful part about her effectiveness is that she is one of the most zealous Christophers you could find. What refreshing hope for the future there will be once thousands more like her dedicate themselves to lifetime careers with similar high purpose.

They will develop together a force for good that nothing will be able to stop, that will sweep over the country and to the farthermost parts of the earth. And, while this is being done, they will gain some inkling of the important roles they are playing in saving the world. It is a knowledge that will buoy them up in the midst of those difficulties which must be the lot of anyone who lives in so intimate a relationship with Christ. His lot was suffering from the Crib to the Cross because He loved even the least of men so much. Those who follow Him on earth must suffer too, but they will see one day what a privilege it was to take things a bit hard here, so that they might make things easier for those who have not been blessed as they have.

TWO MILLION SECRETARIES

In ancient times secretaries were engaged to handle household matters of the aristocracy, act as trusted assistants, and take care of the social and business correspondence incident to their particular employment. It was only with the invention of the typewriter in 1867 that almost all busy men began to engage secretaries. From then until World War I, men monopolized the field. When women were called upon to relieve men for military service, in the first World War and on an ever-increasing scale in World War II, they proved themselves so competent that they actually took over the field. Where there were approximately twenty-one thousand women secretaries in 1890, there are *now* over two million!

This does not mean, however, that a career as a secretary is altogether closed to men. Many outstanding secretarial jobs are male-staffed, and the prestige given to these jobs can readily be judged by the positions such men are offered when their secretaryship is over.

Hundreds of famous writers, journalists, radio commentators, business executives, reporters, statesmen, government officials, lawyers, movie stars—even two former presidents of the United States (Herbert Hoover and Woodrow Wilson)—laid the groundwork for their outstanding careers by first becoming secretaries.

If you are career-minded and have your eyes on one of the main fields of influence, your arrival at the special job at which you are aiming may very well be made easier by traveling the secretarial route. There is no better opportunity to learn a business from the ground up.

While it would obviously be impossible to list all the jobs in the vital fields which secretaries could fill, even a partial listing should give some idea of the wide variety of opportunities for making felt one's influence for good.

EDUCATION: In education, these men, organizations, departments, and offices all require secretarial help:

Board of Education directors
Educational foundations
College departmental heads
College presidents
Placement directors
Board of Examiners
Correspondence-school heads
School principals
School librarians
Literary agents
Textbook writers
Professional speakers

Professional publishers
Civic organizations teachers
National teacher associations
National patriotic organizations
Information services directors
Assistant in child institutions
Adult educational groups
Vocational guidance directors
Community organizers
Textbook publishers
Book editors

Welfare-organization officials
Speakers' bureau
Regional group work programs
Public-education association director
Editor, consumer magazine
Public-library director
Bookstore owner

American loyalty organizations
Public-welfare organizations
Psychologists
Research writers
Young adult programs directors
Parole-board counselors

LABOR: Jobs for Christophers are especially important in the following divisions of the labor field—as secretaries to:

Labor-management relations heads
Trade guilds
National Labor Relations Board
Industrial economist
Personnel directors
Employer-employee consultant
Company house organs
Union publicity director

Director, international, national, or local union
Union officials
Labor leaders
Industrial-relations men
Placement officers
Position classifiers
Labor press
Department of Labor
Union educational directors

COMMUNICATIONS: (Newspapers, magazines, books, radio-television, et cetera.) A few job possibilities in this vital field for the Christopher secretary:

Publishers
Radio station managers
Art directors (large ad agencies)
Book-club executives
Script writers (radio, TV, movies)
House-organ editors
Newsletter editors

Radio-TV package producers
Motion-picture censors
Chiefs, national press services
Writers of comic books
Literary agents
Playwrights
Radio directors
Direct-mail executive
Columnists

Newspaper editors
Copywriter (AAAA Agency)
Personnel directors
Public-relations directors
Advertising executives
Greeting cards manufacturers
Publicity heads
Professional speakers
Motion-picture exhibitors
Commentators
Radio-TV training schools
Book-club judges

Comic-book publishers
Speakers' bureaus
Editors, trade papers
Advertising counselors
National Publicity Council
Newspaper publishers
Production assistants (large ad agency)
Program directors, radio-TV
Industrial-relations directors
Radio producers

2.

It's Hard Work

Secretarial work has often been painted as a glamorous career, but the facts tell a different story. Only one who has had to arrive before the office officially opened in order to rush a vital dispatch into the morning mail—or who has worked far into the night after everyone else has gone home at five—knows what it really means to be a secretary.

There is one quality (aside from loyalty) that all executives prize in their secretaries almost more than anything else—and that is the *willingness to accept responsibility*. Plenty of girls have missed out on good jobs simply by being afraid to assume responsibility. Remember, confidence based on knowledge of one's abilities is an invaluable asset. Build your knowledge of your job soundly, then you'll have no handicapping fears.

When you go to a new job, familiarize yourself with the background of the organization for which you work. Take home the office-procedure book, if one is available. It can be invaluable in acquainting you with other departments, names of executives, employees, and in showing you just how your job and your department fits into the whole picture. Your employer will appreciate your interest.

But a word of warning. Don't start in like a new broom about to sweep clean and endeavor to renovate the office and your employer's working habits. Every employer is different. And it is up to you to adjust yourself to your boss. He may enjoy working with his desk in a state of chaos—or he may expect to start the day with a polished desk, sharpened pencils, and all his papers in order. The best thing to do is ask him what his preferences are and be guided accordingly thereafter.

PRACTICAL SUGGESTIONS

It has already been established that secretarial work can be work with high purpose. As in any other field of endeavor, however, there are many practical suggestions which will go a long way toward helping you make the most effective use of your energies and skill. You should take to heart, therefore, the following guide to better secretarial practice:

1. Don't broadcast your employer's faults to the rest of the office. They are nobody's business but his own—and yours, insofar as they affect your working conditions.

2. Don't indulge in office gossip. Your boss will have a higher regard for you. And you'll have a higher regard for yourself.

3. Keep your personal affairs out of office routine.

4. Use some of your spare time to learn more about your job.

5. Lead a rich, full Christian life, well balanced as regards choice of friends, participation in sports and study groups, protection of health, and, above all, devotion to God. The effects of such a life will be reflected in your work, and your work will be that much the better for it.

6. Don't be afraid to ask for information which will aid you to do a job well. To attempt to bluff out a situation without sufficient knowledge invariably will have unfortunate repercussions—for you.

7. Don't be stymied when someone tells you a thing "just can't be done." If your boss wants it done, busy yourself finding out how it *can be* accomplished. Some way will suggest itself if the problem is approached with thought and perseverance.

8. Accept criticism, if such criticism is really the result of some action or omission on your part. But don't brood over your mistakes. Endeavor to see that they are not repeated.

9. Be cheerful, friendly, and courteous at all times.

10. Accept with good spirit menial, routine jobs, such as addressing envelopes, mailing packages, running errands, et cetera.

THE QUICKEST ROUTE

In addition to these ten suggestions there is one other which will provide the fundamental basis for the eventual success of your program of Christopher action. It is prayer!

Prayer is the quickest means to rediscover your purpose in life. And, once found, prayer will help you to keep that purpose. Since there is a constant temptation to allow one's ambitions to be directed into channels that will do little to bring God-given values into the market place, the secretary who has a Christopher purpose must constantly remind herself that she is working for Christ and not for herself alone.

The importance of this sense of dedication and devotion is evident from what one secretary wrote to us not long ago. *"I just wish I could shout from the housetops the necessity of offering everything you do for the love of God,"* she stated. *"Not only does it increase your own capacity to do good, but it takes the small and petty out of each day. Before, where I was inclined to grumble when a distasteful job came my way, now I actually get a kick out of saying, 'I'm doing this for You, God.' Even on bigger jobs that I might have felt unable to tackle, just as soon as I've said, 'Lord, I can't do this without You'—I get to work. And I can't help feeling that the Lord is pleased to be called on like this, even to help out in office routine, because He's never failed me."*

237

A motivation such as this is indeed a refreshing contrast to that of the godless over the world who see the deified State as the answer to all our ills and who squander their enthusiasm in a materialistic "cause."

A secretary with a Christopher purpose will go out of her way to reach all people. But never will she compromise on fundamentals or back down on matters of faith or morals. Since she has the Truth, she will have the courage to testify to it, even among those who are hostile to it. And the comforting thing for her to remember is that she will not be alone, for *one with God is a majority*. So long as she keeps this thought uppermost in her mind, she will be able to accomplish wonders.

ACTUAL PROOF

In a large southern medical college the secretary to one of the head doctor-instructors has done a tremendous amount of good by the manner in which she has answered her employer's correspondence. Whenever the opportunity arises, and with the doctor's permission, she gently gets across in her letters a strong note of Christian ethical and spiritual concepts. Her job isn't especially highly paid, but because she realizes the good she can do where she is, she wrote to tell us she intends to "stay put." She realizes that because she is there, Christ is there also, working through her as He works through all who would do His Will.

A well-known motion-picture executive has announced on more than one occasion that he values the suggestions of his secretary so highly that he frequently consults her when he is in doubt regarding some movie story his company intends to produce. *"I know all the technical angles and production details, of course,"* he said. *"But this secretary of mine has made a lifetime career of her job, and I found out long ago that she supplies what I lack—a constant, unerring sense of spiritual values. Her advice has never proved wrong in all the time I've known her."*

A secretary employed by a midwestern board of education took the post because he felt he could use his talent and energies to bring Christ into the market place far better there than in some other line of work. In any number of ways he has been able to get across his sound, Christian ideas to the various members of the board. In one particular instance when the board was considering for use in the schools of the community a book that contained strong overtones of atheistic and materialistic philosophy, this young man expressed his opposition so convincingly that the volume was eventually turned down. Furthermore, the head of the board personally extended his thanks for the secretary's interest and concern. *"I wish we had more people like you in our community,"* he told him. *"I've come to the conclusion that we have great need of them."*

One woman, now a leading syndicated newspaper columnist specializing in giving sound advice to young women and girls, began her career as a secretary on a large East Coast daily paper. For years she stayed in the same position, perfecting her skills and absorbing all there was to know about the newspaper business. Then came a small advancement to a more responsible job. She performed her new duties so well that before very much time had passed she was advanced to the next higher position. Finally she was assigned to write a column for the local paper. So strong was her purpose to leave the world better than she found it that everything she wrote reflected her Christopher outlook on life. Today her column goes out to a number of newspapers throughout the country— and with it goes her influence for good. In a very real, constructive sense, she is "reaching for the world" with tremendously encouraging results.

CHANGED ATTITUDE

The attitude possessed by people such as these changed their whole approach to their jobs. They resisted the unfortunate tendency among some in the secretarial field to become too much preoccupied with striving for more and more power, money, and public acclaim for their accomplishments. This tendency has hurt rather than helped them, for, in the long run, it has smothered completely the sensitivity and fine feeling proper to woman.

The qualities of tact, delicacy, and a genuinely warm feeling for *all* humanity are what are needed in the modern world, much more than a cold, impersonal, administrative rigidity. Those secretaries, moreover, who will eventually marry and establish homes and families will have fostered in the meantime the very qualities that will make them happy and successful wives and mothers.

Similarly, those whom God has chosen to remain single, in order to make their personal contribution to the world via a career, will be happier for replacing any tendency to self-love with the soul-satisfying love of God. Day after day they will keep Christ in the market place. They will avoid the "fringes" of everyday living. They will head instead for the *heart* of the great spheres which influence, for better or worse, the destiny not only of the nation but of the world. And they will be adding to, not subtracting from, the sum total of fine, decent, Christian living.

3.

Where To Go

Deciding in which of the vital fields you would like to work is the next step in becoming a secretary with a purpose. To that end, a brief résumé of the situation in the main spheres of influence may help to clarify your thoughts and aid you in your choice.

EDUCATION

On the surface, the Christopher secretary in the educational field does not seem to have the same direct opportunities as does, say, a teacher. Nevertheless, as a secretary to a board of education director, a university departmental head, a textbook publisher, or any one of a host of like positions, her influence can be brought to bear. The more efficient she is, the greater will be the responsibility delegated to her. She may even earn the rank of "unofficial professor," which Miss Mary Alice Reilly won for herself for a lifetime of service at Columbia University. Miss Reilly, who retired on June 30, 1950, at the age of sixty-seven, after having spent thirty-six years as secretary of the university's graduate history department, merited her title by her willingness to type many a student's thesis during her free moments and by her sincere interest in all those with whom she came in contact every day. In fact, according to the account given in the New York *Herald Tribune,* scarcely a morning went by that the mail did not include pictures of some student's fiancée, wife, or latest addition to the family. To Miss Reilly her job was something more than a routine proposition. It was an opportunity to pursue a lifetime of service to the young people of America.

One of the most influential people in the school is the *Secretary to the Board,* who is usually the superintendent's secretary. It is through her that most business is done, and her influence can be and *is* felt by the whole school.

For those who obtain positions as secretaries to textbook publishers, many matters of policy and decision will be left to their discretion. If they are atheistic, it is an easy matter to slip in books that stress their point of view. As men and women with Christopher purpose, it will be similarly easy to encourage, in an honest manner, selection along the lines of Christian thought.

GOVERNMENT

Today, as never before, we need persons of high character and competence to staff our government—federal, state, and local. From the lowliest civil servant on up to the highest, government service is a public trust. The greatest demand for government workers, moreover, *lies in the secretarial field*. More jobs are open in this category than in any other. Secretaries are even employed before they pass a Civil Service examination and are rated. The need is so great that many are hired on a temporary basis and urged to take the next Civil Service test, at which time their tenure will be made permanent.

In the section of this book devoted to Government a detailed listing of the various departments therein will provide a more comprehensive picture of the wealth of opportunities available. We suggest you consult it.

LABOR

The secretary with a sane Christian outlook on social questions can do much good in the labor field—for there, in our present conditions of social and economic life, are the great opportunities for good or evil—and there, more than anywhere else, Christian principles are needed. There will always be areas of difference between employers and employees. However, the Christopher point of view holds that these differences can exist without serious detriment to either side, provided honesty, decency, a sense of fair play, and acknowledgment of man's God-given dignity, rights, and responsibilities are *mutually* recognized. In other words, both sides must play the game according to the rules.

COMMUNICATIONS

Probably there is no greater opportunity to "insist on truth where others are intent on furthering falsehood, to establish order where others are spreading confusion . . . to plant more firmly the fundamentals which others are trying to uproot . . ." than in the field of *Communications*.

CONVEY IDEAS

Conveying ideas is one of the biggest industries in America today. We are influenced by the books, magazines, newspapers, advertisements we read, by the sounds that come over the radio from a script written in advance, by stage plays, by motion pictures, by television, by newsreels. Yet all too frequently each of these media of expression represents a continuous and deliberate appeal to our baser instincts. In the field of *writing* alone, the situation leaves much to be desired. As J. Edgar Hoover, head of the FBI, pointed out: *"Filthy literature is the great moron-maker. It is casting criminals faster than prisons can absorb them."*

Of course, just as Christopher secretaries in the field of education do not have the same opportunities to bring their influence to bear as do Christopher teachers, so the Christopher secretary in the field of communications will not have the same chance to bring Christ into the market place as do writers, directors, editors, reporters, and so on.

Nevertheless, a secretary can do a great deal in the way of stressing positive Christian principles. The secretary to one leading radio executive was instrumental in bringing her employer's attention to the fact that a documentary program aired over his network was following a completely godless, materialistic line. The propaganda was subtle, but since the secretary had access to the scripts she was able to anaylze them in detail and discover what was going on.

She didn't stop there, however. She didn't just complain about what was bad. She tried to replace evil with good. She made it a point to bring to the attention of her employer scripts that stressed sound, truly American ideals.

THE OTHER SIDE OF THE PICTURE

With similar determination, but for a far different purpose, a young Communist secretary in New York took upon herself a rather unusual task. A certain well-known critic was going out of his way consistently to oppose the subversive trend in the literary work, so this girl decided to do something about it. She realized that a post as his secretary offered the best chance to get her atheistic ideas across to him as well as to his readers. The critic already had a secretary, but despite this the young Communist made up her mind that someday she was going to secure the job.

A few people told her it couldn't be done—but eventually she did it. It took quite a while, of course, and she had to take another job while she was waiting, but she didn't become discouraged. She sent in her application, and in her spare time she did everything she could to improve her secretarial efficiency. She left no stone unturned in getting ready for the day when her big chance to "move in" arrived.

And the chance did come. The critic's secretary got married and gave up her position, and this young Communist, because of her purposeful preparation, was chosen above all the other applicants.

She didn't do anything to get her ideas across right away. For some two or three months she concentrated on making the best possible impression on her employer. She gladly worked overtime; nothing was ever too much trouble for her; in general she strove to make her services absolutely indispensable. Naturally she succeeded.

The critic began to give her more and more responsibility. He raved to his friends and associates about what a wonderfully efficient person his secretary was. "Why, she's doing half my work!" he boasted. That's exactly what she was doing: half his work—writing half his column, answering half his letters, seeing half his visitors. As time went on her "literary" contributions became even more pronounced—and more and more slanted according to her ideological sympathies. Imagine the critic's astonishment when an acquaintance at dinner one day asked him just when he had started to embrace the leftist point of view. The critic, of course, denied the charge vehemently. But he did check the contents of his column from then on . . . and soon put a stop to the ideological "sleigh ride" on which his misplaced confidence had taken him.

In a sense, however, the damage already had been done. Countless numbers among his audience undoubtedly had their tastes influenced to some extent even without their realizing it.

A WORD FOR THE BEGINNER

All that has been written so far has been predicated upon your having the technical training necessary to your calling. It is understood that the Christopher secretary will be technically perfect in basic skills (shorthand 100–120 wpm; transcribed at 40–50 wpm; with straight copy typing at a minimum of 60 wpm). She will be expert in grammar, spelling, and English. She will have a practical working knowledge of bookkeeping and will develop a keen memory and liking for system and detail. For those who do not have the technical requirements but are stimulated to seek a secretarial career, the following suggestions are offered:

A school of secretarial practice should be chosen as carefully as you would select a college. Find out a school's rating, study its catalogue, check with some organization like the National Council of Business Schools, Washington 9, D.C.

The *length* of secretarial-school training will depend on how much you want to specialize. There are courses as short as six weeks and there are some as long as four years. An evening course will take longer than a full day course.

A VALUABLE LESSON

To be a secretary with a Christopher purpose means hard work, sufficient preparation, an unflagging perseverance to reach your goal. Constantly before your mind's eye should be the eloquent reminder contained in the Gospel story of Christ and the fig tree which He cursed and caused to wither away, not because it was doing any harm but only *because it was doing no good*. It produced only foliage, not the fruit for which it was created. *"And seeing a certain fig tree by the way side, He came to it, and found nothing on it but leaves only, and He saith to it: May no fruit grow on thee henceforward for ever. And immediately the fig tree withered away."* (Matthew 21:19)

4.

Additional Qualities

In addition to technical proficiency, and a faithful application of all the "do's" and "don't's" which we have listed earlier, there are certain other qualities which you, as a secretary with a Christopher purpose, will find invaluable and which you should cultivate if you do not already possess them.

Be *enthusiastic* about your job. Little that is great was ever accomplished without that quality. Take the case of the zealous radio script writer in the Midwest who started her career as a secretary in a station operated by one of the network chains. Her genuine enthusiasm for her work caught the attention of several of the studio officials. When they learned that she had prepared for a writing career while in college, she was advanced to her present post the very first time an opening in the script department occurred. And here, too, her zeal paid off. Recently she wrote to us, explaining how she had started and built up a radio program which is on the air every Monday through Friday of every week and which, in her own words, is *"strictly a Christopher show, attempting, as it does, to clear up misunderstandings, misconceptions, and the like."*

And she went on to say: *"It has had a success far beyond expectations. One announcement that there was thought of discontinuing it in favor of another network feature brought cards and letters of protest, with long lists of names from all over this area. The show has been a great personal satisfaction to us all. In the beginning certain staff members thought it had little value. We fought for it; and the poll taken proved a point. People DO want to be better. They want what the Christophers have to give. I am personally humbly grateful for being given this comparatively wide-scale means of operation.*

"In the letters we found so many wonderful evidences of influence. One lady said meetings of an organization were now free from petty talk and bickering. Another had been ill and discouraged—in a 'rut.' Still another man said he thought he was doing all right until he listened to the show one morning, quite by chance. Then he realized he led a very narrow life in not getting into community affairs and helping straighten some objectionable things out. He had been, he said, smug in his self-righteous attitude—but he would change all that now into positive, constructive action.

"I'm going to send you a sample script soon. Meanwhile, I'd like to ask your permission to use some of the thoughts in your books. The work of the Christophers CAN be done. I have run into some folks who say it can't. But didn't Our Lord Himself place the responsibility on the individual? There doesn't seem to be a good answer to that one—not from the afore-mentioned folk, anyway. . . ."

IT'S CATCHING!

Remember that if you develop an attitude of *optimism*, others will catch your spirit. A healthy and happy outlook on life is, after all, one of the distinguishing marks of any Christopher. Take pleasure in the joy you can give to others through your positive approach in improving a bad situation instead of wasting all your energies in concentrating on what is wrong.

If you are in one of the creative fields, it is suggested that you try a little "creating" on your own. For instance, draw up your idea of a pamphlet, a promotion campaign letter, a piece of copy—whatever you believe you could do well. Do it on your own time, if necessary, and show it to your boss. Ask for his critical opinion. Tell him you want to learn and would appreciate his guidance. Try to follow the line of your employer's reasoning and parallel his style as nearly as possible. If you can learn to write as he does, he will often give you more and more opportunities to display your talents.

BE "LETTER-PERFECT"

Your knowledge of grammar and sentence construction should be above reproach, but not at the expense of naturalness. Leave your school-day textbook "at home" and make more intelligent use of your knowledge in the office. It is your job, of course, to correct obvious errors; but don't ruin an employer's writing style in an effort to make every sentence conform to rigid literary standards. Many businessmen prefer to write as they would talk, and common practice has made this acceptable. Be governed accordingly.

Another quality that will stand you in good stead is the ability to finish what your employer has started, and this should be accomplished without requiring his constant supervision. To that end, do not merely listen when you are given instructions—listen and think. Visualize the assignment as your employer describes it, and if you have any questions, ask them while his mind is completely centered on the assignment.

DON'T GET LOST IN DETAILS

There will always be something to do around an office, and it will be impossible for you to take on all the tasks without wearing yourself out. Don't get smothered in the details of your job, in trying to take on too much. If you are invested with the authority, delegate as much responsibility as is feasible. There are probably others in the concern who can do many things as efficiently as you can. If you burden yourself with matters which could well be done by someone else, you will only lessen your own effectiveness in dealing with the *really important* details of your daily work. On the other hand, never be above the menial chores which are a part of every job.

KNOW WHERE TO FIND INFORMATION

Knowing where and how to find information is another duty of a secretary which is sometimes neglected by the beginner.

Check on information which is available in the various

directories that are used by your company, and keep up to date on new directories that come out and that might add to the information you already have. Know how to use the classified telephone directory of your locality intelligently, plus special trade directories, social registers, magazines, periodicals, yearbooks, and the like, all of which might prove useful to you in your job. This is a duty for your spare time, so that when the immediate need for certain information arises you will be prepared.

Time spent in developing your "know-how" is almost as important as your formal education. If you aim to go to the top in your chosen field—and there is certainly nothing wrong in such an ambition—every bit of knowledge that will have a bearing on making you more efficient as a secretary will prove invaluable in the long run.

And it follows that if you are a good secretary, the boss will appreciate your opinions because he has seen your good judgment and intelligence in action. With this reputation, the Christopher-minded secretary will be in a position to offer her ideas. Secretaries have many opportunities to "chat with the boss." When an employer feels like talking, the secretary is there.

As one secretary wrote us: "Chats like this often bring on discussions of many subjects on which we do not agree at all. I well remember my first disagreement with my employer. It was on the existence of God. I thought surely he would fire me—but I refused to back down—and he ended up with a greater respect for me. In fact, he remarked that I was the first person he had met in ten years who cared enough about the subject even to discuss it. And I am sure this obtains in a great many secretarial jobs. The solution is to take advantage of the opportunity to speak your piece—and speak it so plainly that nobody is in the dark as to where you stand. Sooner or later, if you and your boss are poles apart on basic ideas, you're going to have to stand up and be counted. Against that day, you have got to prepare yourself to give good reason for the things in which you believe. Once having given that reason, you can expect that your beliefs will frequently be challenged, which is really a compliment, since the assumption is that you stand for something positive."

GROUNDWORK FOR THE FUTURE

There is another important job a secretary can do, even though she plans to work at her present job only a comparatively short period of time.

Your present employer undoubtedly will go on working for the better part of his life, and while he may not be prominent or important *now,* there is a good chance he will be a person of considerable influence in the future. The idea, then, is to bring your Christopher approach into your association with him while you have the opportunity. With God's grace, you may succeed in sharing your ideals with him far more than you know. And just think what you will have accomplished! Men who will, perhaps, determine the policy of radio or television networks, publishing houses, labor unions, government departments, educational institutions, and the like, may owe much of their firm grounding in God-given principles to you. If you are zealous *and* tactful, you can be responsible for forming many of the thinking habits of those who may shape the destiny of our country and the world in the years to come.

TIME TO ACT

The situation of the world today, while desperate, does *not* call for hysterical outbursts of emotion. Rather does it call for grim, apostolic determination of the part of all Christophers, secretaries included. Those who would truly bear Christ into the market place must work as hard to integrate spiritual values into all phases of life, even as the enemies of God and mankind are striving to eliminate them. *Your* action, therefore, should be *positive* action, in the spirit of the thought so well expressed by Pope Pius XI, when he said:

"We cherish the firm hope that the fanaticism with which the sons of darkness work day and night at their materialistic and atheistic propaganda will at least serve the holy purpose

of stimulating the sons of light to a like and even greater zeal for the honor of the Divine Majesty."

FOR ADDITIONAL READING

DOUTT, HOWARD M. *Secretarial Science*. Chicago: Richard D. Irwin, 1942.

PAINTOR and MONRO. *Secretary's Handbook*. New York: Macmillan, 1950; 6th edition.

PRATT, MARGARET. *The Successful Secretary*. New York: Lothrop, Lee & Shepard, 1946; illustrated by Roger Duvoisin. P. 144.

SCOTT, LOUISE HOLLISTER and ELIZABETH CORSON BELCHER. *How to Get a Secretarial Job*. New York: Harper & Brothers, 1942. Pp. v + 104.

TURNER, BERNICE C. *The Private Secretary's Manual*. New York: Prentice-Hall, 1949; revised.

Standard Handbook for Secretaries. New York: McGraw-Hill, 1949; 5th edition.